EAT THE POSSUM
CONQUERING LIFE'S TOUGHEST CHALLENGES ONE BITE AT A TIME

DR. JOHN UTLEY

EAT THE POSSUM
By Dr. John Utley
©2025 All Rights Reserved

Cotton House Press Books are published by
Cotton House Press LLC
640 Taylor Street, Suite 1200
Fort Worth, Texas 76102
Visit our website at www.cottonhouse.press

Eat The Possum: Conquering Life's Toughest Challenges One Bite at a Time

Copyright © 2024 by Dr. John Utley

All rights reserved.

No part of this publication may be reproduced, distributed, or transmitted in any form or by any means, including photocopying, recording, or other electronic or mechanical methods, without the prior written permission of the publisher, except in the case of brief quotations embodied in critical reviews and certain other noncommercial uses permitted by copyright law.

Unless otherwise indicated, all Scripture quotations are taken from the *Holy Bible*, New Living Translation, copyright © 1996, 2004, 2015 by Tyndale House Foundation. Used by permission of Tyndale House Publishers, Carol Stream, Illinois 60188. All rights reserved. Scripture taken from the Amplified Bible (AMPCE), Copyright © 1954, 1958, 1962, 1964, 1965, 1987 by The Lockman Foundation. Used by permission. Scriptures taken from the Holy Bible, New International Version®, NIV®. Copyright © 1973, 1978, 1984, 2011 by Biblica, Inc.™ Used by permission of Zondervan. All rights reserved worldwide. www.zondervan.com The "NIV" and "New International Version" are trademarks registered in the United States Patent and Trademark Office by Biblica, Inc.™ Scripture quotations marked "ESV" are taken from The ESV® Bible (The Holy Bible, English Standard Version®), © 2001 by Crossway, a publishing ministry of Good News Publishers. Used by permission. All rights reserved. Scripture quotations marked (KJV) are taken from the Authorized (King James) Version. Rights in the Authorized Version in the United Kingdom are vested in the Crown. Reproduced by permission of the Crown's patentee, Cambridge University Press.

Eat The Possum: Conquering Life's Toughest Challenges One Bite at a Time

ISBN: 979-8-9897607-5-6 (Hardback)
979-8-9897607-6-3 (Paperback)
979-8-9897607-7-0 (EPub)

979-8-9897607-8-7 (Audio Book)
Library of Congress Control Number: 2024952051
Printed in United States of America
First Edition: February 2, 2025

Cover design and interior formatting by *Hannah Linder Designs*

To Susan, my rock and my muse, who never flinched at the thought of barbecued marsupials.

To my children, Joanna, Bobby, Jonathan, Jordan, Joshua and Chelsea, who cheered me on even when Dad's ideas seemed a bit wild.

To Gerald, Debora, Elizabeth, Rebekah and Vera who nurtured my dreams from backyard critters to life-changing metaphors.

And to my best friends, Tim and Debbie, true friends and fellow adventurers, who never hesitated to join me on crazy adventures.

You all taught me that sometimes, the most profound wisdom comes from unexpected places. This one's for you—with all my love and a side of BBQ sauce.

CONTENTS

Introduction	ix
1. EYEBALL TO EYEBALL WITH YOUR POSSUM	1
2. POSSUM-SIZED COURAGE	23
3. SNIFFING OUT YOUR PERSONAL POSSUM	41
4. ASSEMBLING YOUR POSSUM-HUNTING POSSE	55
5. LIGHTING A FIRE UNDER YOUR POSSUM'S TAIL	69
6. SAVORING THE POTENTIAL AROMA OF VICTORY	79
7. POSSUM PICNIC: SPREADING THE FEAST AND TAKING NAMES	99
8. POSSUM POTLUCK: SHARING YOUR CATCH	113
9. TENDERIZING TOUGH POSSUM MEAT	127
10. POSSUM PARTY: TOASTING YOUR TRIUMPH	141
11. RIDING THE POSSUM WAVE	153
12. FROM POSSUM TO PLATYPUS: DREAMING BIGGER	181
Possum Notes	191
Possum Pickin's: Finger-Lickin' Recipes for Your Next Roadkill Rodeo	227
Eat The Possum Personality Quiz	233
About the Author	239

INTRODUCTION

In human experience, where the landscapes of our challenges loom large and daunting, there lies an untold story of triumph and tenacity. It's a narrative that unfolds in the heart of anyone who has ever stood before their personal Goliath and whispered, "It's too hard." This battle is not just a story of overcoming; it is an odyssey that traverses the rugged terrains of the soul, where every setback, every defeat, harbors the seeds of potential victory. This is the essence of *Eat the Possum: Conquering Life's Toughest Challenges One Bite at a Time*.

Our journey through life is often punctuated by encounters with seemingly insurmountable obstacles. These moments test our resolve, challenge our faith, and question our capacity for endurance. They are the mountains we're hesitant to climb, the giants we're too intimidated to confront. In these encounters, we find ourselves teetering on the brink of resignation, succumbing to a defeat that's more self-imposed than real. We convince ourselves the battle is lost even before it has even begun.

Yet, what if the narrative could change? What if, instead of retreating, we chose to engage; instead of defeat, we embraced the possibility of triumph? This book is about such a shift in perspective. It's about transforming our, "It's too hard," into, "I can conquer." It's about realizing that the most significant victories are often wrapped in the guise of our greatest challenges.

Eating a possum serves as a powerful reminder that overcoming our challenges often requires us to do things we'd never imagined doing. It's about stepping out of our comfort zones, facing our fears, and embracing the unfamiliar with courage and conviction. The story of attending a wild game barbecue in a small farming town, where the idea of eating barbecued possum first seemed repulsive, becomes a profound lesson in confronting and overcoming our biases and fears.

So, I encourage you to view this book as a guide, a companion, a cookbook filled with recipes, and a mentor for anyone who feels overwhelmed by their possums—those daunting challenges that life throws our way. Through personal anecdotes, biblical wisdom, practical advice, and solid research, it aims to equip you with the tools needed to face your fears, overcome your obstacles, and transform your challenges into triumphs.

As you turn these pages, I invite you to embark on this journey with an open heart and a willing spirit. Let the stories, lessons, and insights within inspire you to confront your possums, do the hard things, and discover the strength, resilience, and grace already within you.

Welcome to the journey of overcoming the hardest things in your life. Welcome to the journey of eating the possum.

#eatthepossum

CHAPTER ONE
EYEBALL TO EYEBALL WITH YOUR POSSUM

"It's too hard."

We've all said it when facing massive mountains, standing before intimidating giants, and encountering other complicated things. We've resigned ourselves to the inevitable reality that we will fail to conquer the most challenging thing, even before we begin. After a while, a weird mix of failure and justification creates the feeling that it is okay to lose the battle. We tried with all our strength, but still could not overcome it. Or, worse, we ignored that complicated thing, but it did not go away.

Unfortunately, it also left us with a sense of despondency; relationships never reaching their best place, always coming up short on the budget, those addictions lingering. Something was left undone. Even worse, it may leave us hindered by an obstacle that refuses a breakthrough and the dream of a better life unfulfilled. It may even seep into other areas of life, where failure breeds failure, and eventually, all challenging situations become obstacles to success for anything. Molehills become mountains by our own thinking or our lack of victory.

What if that all changed? What if the most challenging things in your life now became the object of your most significant victory? Imagine life without giants hurling the taunt of failure in your direction. Think of what life would be like if you succeeded in the very area that currently seems to be impossible. Imagine what that would do to future overwhelming obstacles.

That is the purpose of this book. The keys found here can help you overcome the most complex, most challenging problems and prepare you for even more significant victories in the future. But beware—you may have to eat a few barbecued possums along the way.

So, I am going to encourage you to eat the possum!

#eatthepossum

What in the backwoods of Arkansas does that even mean?

My story started a long time ago. My wife and I pastored a church in a small farming town. A farmer named Cletus (nicknamed "Taterbug," no kidding) invited us to attend a wild game barbecue they held in honor of the farmers in the area who bought seed from a local seed company.

As we stepped into the expansive seed company warehouse, our senses were immediately enveloped in a tapestry of sights and aromas that told the story of the wilderness and culinary adventure before us. There was a vibrant buzz of excitement as family and friends by the hundreds gathered around long, checkered-clothed tables just a few feet from multiple buffet stations laden with an array of wild game dishes.

The air was heavy with the rich, smokey scent of barbecue, along with the aromas emanating from the smokers and grills just outside of the warehouse, each manned by an apron-clad smoking enthusiast, contributing to the complex fragrance of grilled raccoon, the gamey fragrance of venison, and other enticing smells of the wild game we were about to consume.

You could tell there was a sense of pride that accompanied this unforgettable tradition that harkened back decades. It was a testament to the community's bond with the farmers and the land, set against the backdrop of a quieter business of seeds and agriculture. We were blessed to enjoy such a moment.

As we moved our way through the line, my anticipation for what was to come was filled with expectation of delicious entrées, including venison, raccoon, muskrat, squirrel, goose, rabbit, wild boar, rattlesnake, and opossum. Even though the technical term for the North American species of marsupials is "opossum," the farmers simply called them "possums."

Our host promptly joined us in line, encouraging us to enjoy our meal. I was eager to fill my plate with the various offerings—until I reached the barbecued possum meat. That's when I said, rather loudly and proudly with a southern twang, "I ain't about to eat no roadkill. No, sir, no possum for me."

It's not because I have anything against possums. I don't know any personally, but there have been a few times when I have crossed paths with a possum. Once, when we were living in Baton Rouge, Louisiana, I caught one rifling through our trash. This possum was taking what it wanted and littering the porch and yard with the rest. I tried to scare it away, but it turned toward me and hissed, showing me its intimidating sharp teeth. I said, "Oh no, Buster, you are not going to get away with littering my backyard with the trash you dug out of my garbage can." He hissed again. I ran into the house, found a broom, and faced it again. He hissed a third time, so I gently pushed it with the brush end. With that light push, it rolled off the porch into the yard. Once it stopped rolling, it was on its back with its tongue hanging out of its mouth. It did not move at all. I ran into the house and called for my wife to come and witness the possum that I had just killed. She ran to see, but by the time she arrived, my "dead" possum had already turned over and shuffled off to another trash can adventure. It was not dead; it was *playing* dead, almost as fast as people play dead when the pastor announces a church workday or prayer meeting.

I have also witnessed the lowly possum lumbering across a road, oblivious to oncoming traffic. And I have often met many possums in their more natural state: as roadkill after said lumbering.

Needless to say, while possum may have been on the menu at the seed company's wild game barbecue, it was not on mine.

My host, however, heard my loud bantering about "roadkill" and decided to take matters into his own hands. Evidently, one never says "never" to Cletus. I liken it to telling God what you will not do and then finding out that you must face precisely what you declared to be off-limits. If you tell God that you will never do something, He will call you to do the never you never ever wanted to do. In fact, after you say never, you will be nevering like you have never nevered before. I have had that happen too often, yet I still haven't learned to keep "never" out of my vocabulary and prayers.

After I sat down with my heaping plate of wild game barbecue and started eating, Cletus walked up, pushed an equally heaping plate in front of me, and said, "Here is your possum, Preacher."

I rebelled. "I am not going to eat any possum meat, because I don't like roadkill."

His stern response caught me off-guard. "EAT THE POSSUM."

I have to confess that this particular church was difficult for pastors. It took a long time to establish rapport with the locals; outsiders were rarely welcome. My wife and I felt this invitation was a step in the right direction. I certainly did not want to alienate Cletus. Still, I looked at him and said, "I am *not* going to eat the possum."

This time, his response took the form of a command, "EAT THE POSSUM." I looked at him, then at the plate, then back at Cletus with a puzzled look. At that moment, I wondered if this was some hazing or a test to determine if I belonged to the clan. While I contemplated the situation, I did as I always do; I made jokes about rabies and roadkill, wondering aloud which farmer "hunted the varmint down and bagged him."

I laughed, and again, he commanded, "EAT THE POSSUM."

I looked at the heaping plate with an odd aroma and thought, *I am going to be sick.*

My mind was searching for some context of how this was going to end. My very helpful brain landed on a memory from a mission trip to Ecuador years earlier. We were with a team of medical professionals hosting a free medical clinic for a local underserved community. While there, the locals "blessed" us with a farm-raised, highly fattened guinea pig (think of the guinea pig in your local pet store and add about twenty pounds to it). It was huge, and, according to our host for the team, eating its meat would leave one extremely ill. Even though he cautioned against eating it, one team member decided he could not offend the locals. His attempt at appeasement went horribly wrong, and he spent the rest of the week in his hotel room.

I did not want this encounter to result in "possum revenge," confined to home for the rest of the week, either.

My thoughts wandered at that point as I looked at the barbecue meat in front of me. Suddenly, my thoughts were interrupted by a chant. Members of my church and other nameless individuals gathered around my table, chanting, "EAT THE POSSUM," repeatedly.

I seriously considered an exit strategy as they continued to repeat in an ever-increasing crescendo, "EAT THE POSSUM! EAT THE POSSUM! EAT THE POSSUM!"

At the moment, the hardest thing in my life was confronting myself with the gentle aroma of Memphis-style BBQ sauce laced with an uncertain smell of meat.

"EAT THE POSSUM," they chanted over and over again.

I looked at them, and I looked at the plate. I was between a rock and roadkill.

It was then that I seriously wondered why I had accepted the assignment at this church, why anyone would be so adamant about my food choices, and if I really needed to gain their trust. I also thought this was a strange way to treat a guest, pastor, or anyone you cared about. I looked at the choir around me, chanting, Cletus smirking, as my wife raised her eyebrows while rolling her eyes and thinking I had fallen into a wormhole of societal mutation.

At the moment, it was the hardest thing I had to do. It was hard to envision eating this potentially distasteful meat, and, even more so, feeling like I had no choice.

That's when Cletus said something I will never forget: "There is a trick to eating opossum, and it is the same as facing the hardest things in your life. If you learn how to do it, you will eat some great barbecue, and you may also win at life. But if you shy away from this small challenge, the next hard thing may become overwhelming."

"What do you mean?"

He said, "If a simple plate of barbecue stands in your way of great food, what else will you miss out on that lies ahead? A simple taste of this delicacy might just lead you to tackle more difficult things in your future, maybe helping you overcome some of life's biggest obstacles."

I thought about what he said, and the profound effect it had on me was unrealized at the moment, but it did begin a journey of facing the most challenging things in my life with expectancy.

What about you? What is the hardest thing you have ever faced?

There is a story in the Bible, found in Mark 10:17-27, where a rich young ruler approached Jesus, wanting to know what he had to do to get to heaven. It was a great question, and Jesus answered by pointing to the commandments. The ruler noted that he had complied with them all. Jesus told this wealthy man to sell all his possessions, give the money to the poor, and follow Him.

The man was saddened when he left Jesus, because what Jesus commanded was too hard for him.

Most people do not think much of the story, because they are not that wealthy. They struggle from week to week and pay for most things in installments. One surprise expense can sidetrack or destroy them financially. So, for them, this story does not apply to their lives, because they are not rich. They may even mock the rich man for his trust in wealth.

But think of the rich ruler. The most difficult thing in his life was the challenge brought by Jesus to sell it all and follow the Lord. When confronted with this challenge, he walked away. He failed to do the hard thing.

It was simply too hard for him. The hardest thing in his life would challenge everything he held dear.

Now, put yourself in the place of the rich man, not in the same way and not with wealth, but in confronting and overcoming the most challenging thing in your life. What if he had agreed to do as Jesus commanded? I believe he would have experienced an extraordinary life that he could never have had even with all the wealth in the world. Imagine the future breakthroughs that conquering the most challenging thing in his life would have made possible. Imagine walking side-by-side with the Savior of mankind as He healed the sick, raised the dead, walked on water, etc.

Numerous individuals in Scripture failed to overcome complex challenges. However, Scripture also records those who obeyed and found tremendous success despite insurmountable obstacles. What is the difference?

The difference was in their decision to "eat the possum."

Sometimes, we are one challenging thing away from experiencing breakthroughs in other areas of struggle. Winning these battles will encourage more significant victories that may have remained elusive in the past. That roadblock, wall, or let's call it, "roadkill," keeps us from it.

So, here is my challenge to you:

EAT THE POSSUM.
DO THE HARD THING!

What is your hard thing?

Is it forgiving someone who has hurt you?
Is it walking away from a toxic relationship?
Is it tithing for the first time?
Is your hard thing loving someone you don't want to love?
Is your hard thing learning something new, stepping out in faith, or serving God in a place that scares you to death?
Is it going back to college, confronting your spouse over an addiction, reestablishing a relationship with your child, or going to a counselor to repair your marriage?
Is it coming clean to others about a secret in your life?
Is it taming the family budget, or saying no to someone?
Is it getting healthier, losing weight, or overcoming a habit or addiction?
Is your hard thing a business idea you have had for a long time but never acted on?

Maybe your hard thing is that you are spiritually stuck and can't get ahead.

Your hard thing is your possum, and I can tell you that doing the hard thing is not as complicated as it seems.

You are likely thinking, "I DON'T WANT TO EAT A POSSUM." I can relate completely.

Let's not get hung up on the "eating possum" concept right now. Think about the lowly possum for a second—the actual animal in your backyard. Confronting one is scary. Possums have sharp teeth and piercing, beady eyes. They have claws, growl, hiss and can be very intimidating. Hitting one while driving can damage your car. They can crouch and slink. They can quickly run away if they want to but aren't afraid of staring down a threat.

Most people think of possums as I did, but there are misconceptions about possums. For example, some believe they are giant rats. They are not; they are marsupials. Some believe they carry rabies, but it is almost impossible for opossums to have rabies. People think they attack humans, but they do not. They act tougher than they are and, when provoked, will likely faint. They are not playing dead; they are just more afraid of you than you are of them. The greatest misconception is that possums live far away from people. There are likely possums within a short distance of your home. Those misconceptions mirror our illusions about the hard things in our lives. Those hard things may seem scary, hiss and growl, and are closer to you than you know, but they are not nearly as distasteful as you imagine.

Here is the thing: if you do not deal with your possum, it will continue to afflict your life. It will have baby possums that will hang on to the momma possum and create chaos in your life. Those baby possums will have baby possums of their own until there are more possums than you could ever count. Leave the hard thing for another day, and it will likely grow in its ability to intimidate you in other areas of your life.

Recently, a friend shared that she and her husband had lived in a mobile home. One day, the husband opened the pantry only to discover a possum on the floor eating their cornflakes. The husband screamed, closed the door, and ran for a knife. My friend warned him that killing it would get blood everywhere, so he relented. The possum and most cornflakes were missing when he opened the door again. A week later, he opened a dresser drawer in the bedroom, and a baby possum was in the drawer. They moved a few days later.

Like the lowly possum that refuses to leave, your "hard thing" will likely get into your business. It will invade your life, get into your stuff, and eat your cornflakes. It will keep you from victory.

On the contrary, whatever your hard thing is, whatever your possum, victory over it will position you for future success, and that will communicate to the other possums: *I am coming for you, and I'm hungry.*

THE "YOU" FACTOR

Before you delve into the delicious plate of BBQ possum, you have to stop for a moment and consider what I call the "you" factor. Before you attempt the big thing, you have to take a step back and consider how "you" relate to your hard thing. In life, if you are like most people, you struggle with weaknesses, and in the case of your personal possum, something that you have not been able to overcome. The inability to overcome it may be a very tender place in your life, informing all other obstacles. That nagging voice in your head may even remind you of your failure to overcome and cause debilitation in other areas. Even if it is subtle, it can cause you to feel so imperfect that you lose the drive to overcome it. That's part of the "you" factor, because "you" factor into every equation in your life. (They call me Captain Obvious for this insightful insight.)

Let me explain it this way: Scripture says you are fearfully and wonderfully made (Psalm 139:14). It also says we are made in the image of God (Genesis 1:26-31; Colossians 3:10; Genesis 9:6; Genesis 5:1-2; Ephesians 4:24; 1 Corinthians 11:7), which is pretty amazing. But sin marred that image, so our sin keeps us from experiencing the full blessing of walking with God. Sin can potentially inform every area of our life, but so does Christ. The Word of God declares that when we come to Christ, we are no longer orphans but become the children of God: sons and daughters of God. We have all the rights and privileges pertaining to His children. The blessing of this is immeasurable. But even though we know our status and do our best to walk as children of the light, we are still marred. We are weak and need the strength that God has for us. We find that weakness when we attempt to overcome the hardest things in our lives. Even though we are fearfully and wonderfully made, our personality trait(s) may be what has stopped us from victory over our possum in the past.

How does our personality get in the way of overcoming our problem? Different traits can either facilitate or hinder our ability to tackle challenges. For example, a rigid thinker may struggle with adaptability and struggle to adjust to new situations or consider alternate solutions. This will lead the rigid thinker to miss opportunities and increase stress. Impatient individuals may make hasty decisions or lack thoroughness in their plan to overcome their obstacles. Fearful people could be paralyzed from moving forward, which will cause them to miss goals. It will also make them less confident.

In their research, Yiannis Koutras and Stavri Chrysostomou noted, "specific aspects of personality and impulsivity are relevant to weight loss maintenance and should be considered when developing weight management interventions."[1] Other research (found at the back of the book) provided a significant correlation between personality type and the ability to change.

As you can see, different personality traits can undermine one's ability to overcome, but that is not the worst news ever. In fact, it can be the most enlightening news you have heard since you heard the gospel. You were made "You," and your environment, hurts, and traumas have made you distinctly you. Coming to terms with your "you" factor will help you leverage it for victory. Your weaknesses have the potential to become the fulcrum for your victory. This is where the "you" factor gets

---

1. Yiannis Koutras, Stavroula Chrysostomou, Konstantina Giannakou, Mary H. Kosmidis, and Mary Yannakoulia, "Personality Traits and Weight Loss Maintenance: A Cross-Sectional Study," Frontiers in Nutrition 8 (2021): 702382, https://doi.org/10.3389/fnut.2021.702382.

exciting. But first you have to determine what personality type fits you best.

As you read through the following traits, note the individuals who closely align with your traits. You will use this information later in the book. As an added bonus, the personality types of biblical characters are included in the different traits.

To gain a deeper understanding of your personality type, you have several options:

1. Take the personality test provided at the end of this book.
2. Complete the assessment in the *Workbook and Possum Journal* (sold separately).
3. Visit www.eatthepossum.com to access a free online version of the test.

These resources will help you identify your personality traits and how they relate to overcoming challenges.

EAT THE POSSUM PERSONALITIES:

ANALYTICAL ALEX (THINKER):

You're the person who always sees multiple angles to every situation. Your mind is constantly buzzing with ideas and possibilities, making you an excellent problem-solver. However, you often find yourself caught in a web of endless analysis, struggling to make decisions. To leverage your strengths, create a structured decision-making framework with clear deadlines. This will help you channel your analytical prowess into actionable insights, propelling you forward in your personal growth journey. The apostle Paul exemplifies this type. He was highly analytical, logical in his arguments, and adept at critical thinking. His epistles demonstrate complex theological reasoning and strategic planning for church growth.

PRINCIPLED PAULA (PERSISTER):

Your unwavering commitment to your values is both your greatest strength and your biggest challenge. You stand firm in your beliefs, which gives you a strong moral compass. However, this can sometimes make you resistant to change. To grow, identify principles that support personal development and apply your dedication to upholding these new growth-oriented values. This way, you can evolve while staying true to your core beliefs. Daniel fits this type well. He stood firm in his convictions and values, even in the face of persecution. His unwavering commitment to his principles is evident throughout the book of Daniel.

EMPATHETIC EMMA (HARMONIZER):

Your ability to understand and connect with others is remarkable. You're often the glue that holds relationships together. However, your tendency to prioritize others' needs can lead to neglecting your own growth. Reframe personal development as a way to better support and understand those around you. By growing yourself, you'll be even more equipped to help others, creating a positive cycle of mutual growth and understanding. Mary, the mother of Jesus, displays these traits. She showed great empathy and care for others, as seen in her visit to Elizabeth and her concern at the wedding in Cana.

CHARISMATIC CHARLIE (PROMOTER):

Your enthusiasm is contagious, and you have a knack for inspiring others. You thrive on new experiences and are always ready for the next adventure. However, this can sometimes lead to a lack of follow-through on long-term goals. To leverage your strengths, break down your objectives into exciting short-term challenges. Use your persuasive skills to create accountability partnerships, turning your personal growth into a shared, motivating experience. The apostle Peter embodies this type. He was outgoing, enthusiastic, and often the first to speak or act among the disciples.

Spontaneous Sam (Rebel):

You're the free spirit who thrives on breaking norms and challenging the status quo. Traditional approaches to personal growth might feel stifling to you. Embrace your rebellious nature by designing unconventional, creative methods for self-improvement. View personal change as a form of rebellion against your current limitations, turning growth into an exciting act of defiance. Samson fits this profile. He was known for his impulsive actions and disregard for conventional rules.

Contemplative Cory (Imaginer):

Your rich inner world is a source of incredible creativity and insight. You can envision detailed scenarios of personal growth with ease. However, you might struggle with translating these visions into reality. Bridge this gap by setting small, achievable goals that align with your imagined future. Use your visualization skills to maintain motivation and create a clear path from imagination to action. John, the beloved disciple, aligns with this type. His gospel and letters reveal a deeply contemplative and visionary nature.

Ambitious Ava (Achiever):

Your drive for success is unparalleled. You set high standards for yourself and consistently push to meet them. However, this relentless pursuit can lead to burnout if not balanced with self-care. Redefine success to include personal well-being, setting goals for self-care and personal growth with the same intensity as your professional objectives. Remember: a well-rounded life is the ultimate achievement. Nehemiah demonstrates these traits. He set ambitious goals for rebuilding Jerusalem's walls and worked tirelessly to achieve them.

INTUITIVE IAN (DISCERNER):

Your intuition gives you a unique perspective on personal growth, allowing you to see patterns and possibilities others might miss. However, your perfectionism can lead to procrastination. Embrace imperfection as part of the growth process, using your intuition to identify the most impactful areas for development. Trust your inner guidance while taking concrete steps towards your goals. The prophet Jeremiah fits this profile. He had deep insights into spiritual matters and was sensitive to God's leading.

ADVENTUROUS ANDY (EXPLORER):

Your love for new experiences makes life an exciting journey of discovery. You're always ready to try something new, which can be a powerful tool for personal growth. However, maintaining consistency in long-term pursuits can be challenging. Frame your personal development as a thrilling expedition of self-discovery. Create varied, novel approaches to keep your interest piqued in long-term goals. Abraham exemplifies this type. He left his homeland to follow God's call, embracing new experiences and challenges.

CAUTIOUS CATHY (QUESTIONER):

Your skeptical nature and attention to detail make you an excellent researcher. You don't accept ideas at face value, preferring to dig deep and understand the underlying principles. Use these strengths to thoroughly investigate and customize growth strategies. Embrace your skepticism as a tool for finding truly effective methods, creating a personal development plan that stands up to your rigorous standards. Thomas, the disciple, aligns with this profile. He was skeptical and needed evidence before believing in Jesus' resurrection.

DIPLOMATIC DAN (PEACEMAKER):

Your ability to see all sides of a situation and find common ground is a rare gift. You excel at creating harmony in your environment. However, this can sometimes lead to avoiding necessary conflicts or changes. Reframe personal growth as a way to create long-term harmony, both internally and in your relationships. Use your conflict resolution skills to navigate internal resistance to change, finding a peaceful path to personal development. Barnabas fits this type. He often played the role of mediator and encourager in the early Church.

ORGANIZED OLIVIA (GUARDIAN):

Your attention to detail and love for structure make you incredibly efficient and reliable. You thrive on routines and clear expectations. Apply these strengths to your personal growth by creating detailed, structured plans for development. Use your respect for authority to seek guidance from respected mentors or experts, incorporating their wisdom into your well-organized approach to self-improvement. Esther demonstrates these traits. She carefully planned and executed her strategy to save her people.

VISIONARY VICTOR (INNOVATIVE THINKER):

Your innovative thinking and ability to see multiple perspectives make you a natural problem-solver and idea generator. However, focusing on one area of growth at a time can be challenging. Leverage your unique abilities by creating interconnected growth strategies that stimulate your need for variety. Embrace your multi-faceted approach as a tool for comprehensive personal development, allowing you to grow in multiple areas simultaneously. Moses aligns with this type. He had a grand vision for leading the Israelites to freedom and establishing them as a nation.

SUPPORTIVE SARAH (COUNSELOR):

Your natural inclination to help others makes you an invaluable friend and colleague. You have a gift for understanding people's needs and providing emotional support. However, this can sometimes lead to neglecting your own growth. Apply your counseling skills to yourself, creating a personal development plan that aligns with your values of supporting others. Priscilla, who, along with her husband, Aquila, mentored and supported many in the early Church, fits this profile.

As you can see, the "You Factor" isn't as bad as you thought, but it may be the very thing that has hindered your victory before. While each personality type has weaknesses, leveraging your personality type to your benefit puts you in places that biblical characters have trod. You are on amazing ground, and if I can dare say it, in the presence of awesome barbeque possum. Take note of the personality type that closely resembles yours, as we will discuss each one later in the book.

That brings me to this point and the reason for this book; it is to help you "Eat the Possum." It is a recipe for successfully dealing with the most challenging things in your life. We will teach you how to eat possums (recipes included), and, once you determine your "you" factor, you must do the next most challenging thing: Identify Your Possum. While exercises are included in this book, the *Workbook and Possum Journal* (sold separately) is a great aid to help you in your possum eating journey.

POSSUM DISCOVERY EXERCISE

STEP 1: REFLECTION

Take a few minutes to reflect on your life. Think about areas where you've said or thought, "It's too hard." List these areas below:

STEP 2: IMPACT ASSESSMENT

For each item on your list, rate its impact on your life from 1 (minimal impact) to 5 (significant impact):

1. _____ (1-5)
2. _____ (1-5)
3. _____ (1-5)
4. _____ (1-5)
5. _____ (1-5)

Step 3: Frequency Check

How often do you encounter or think about each challenge? Rate from 1 (rarely) to 5 (constantly):

1. _____ (1-5)
2. _____ (1-5)
3. _____ (1-5)
4. _____ (1-5)
5. _____ (1-5)

Step 4: Emotional Response

How does each challenge make you feel? Write one or two emotions for each:

Step 5: Avoidance Patterns

Have you been avoiding or procrastinating on any of these challenges? Mark Yes or No:

1. Yes / No
2. Yes / No
3. Yes / No
4. Yes / No
5. Yes / No

Step 6: Identifying Your Possum

Look at your responses. The challenge with the highest impact, frequency, emotional response, and avoidance is likely your primary "possum." Write it here:

My Possum: _____

Step 7: Possum Characteristics

Describe your possum. What makes it challenging? Why have you avoided it?

Step 8: Potential Benefits

If you were to overcome this possum, what benefits might you experience?

Step 9: Commitment

Are you ready to face your possum? Write a brief commitment statement:

I commit to facing my possum _____ by:

_____
Sign here

Remember, identifying your possum is the first step towards overcoming it. Keep this exercise handy as you continue reading *Eat the Possum* for strategies to tackle your challenge.

FACING YOUR POSSUM QUESTIONS

1. How has your perception of your biggest challenge (your "possum") changed after reading this chapter? What new insights have you gained about facing difficult tasks?
2. Reflect on a time when you've said, "It's too hard," in the past. How might your life be different if you had chosen to "eat the possum" instead?
3. Consider your personality type as identified in the chapter. How might your specific traits both help and hinder you in facing your biggest challenges?
4. How can you reframe your "It's too hard" mindset into an "I can conquer" attitude? What specific steps can you take to shift your perspective?
5. Think about a biblical character who faced a seemingly insurmountable challenge. How can their story inspire you to face your own "possum"?
6. If you know what your "possum" is, what is the greatest challenge facing you as you attempt to "eat the possum?"

A SUMMARY OF CHAPTER 1 OF *EAT THE POSSUM*:

- The chapter introduces the concept of facing difficult challenges, metaphorically referred to as "eating the possum."
- It begins with a personal anecdote about the author's experience at a wild game barbecue, where he was pressured to eat barbecued possum.

- The story serves as an analogy for confronting life's most challenging obstacles.
- The author emphasizes that avoiding difficult tasks can lead to a cycle of failure and missed opportunities.
- A biblical example of the rich young ruler is used to illustrate how failing to do the "hard thing" can result in missing out on greater blessings.
- The chapter challenges readers to identify their own "possum"— their most difficult challenge or obstacle.
- It introduces the "you" factor, emphasizing how personality traits can influence one's ability to overcome challenges.
- Various personality types are described, each with biblical character examples, to help readers identify their own traits.
- The chapter includes a "Possum Discovery Exercise" to help readers identify their primary challenge.
- It concludes by encouraging readers to commit to facing their "possum" and overcome their biggest obstacles.
- The overall message is that confronting and overcoming difficult challenges can lead to personal growth and future successes.

CHAPTER TWO
POSSUM-SIZED COURAGE
FACING YOUR FEARS HEAD-ON

L et's talk about the secret sauce that makes facing your fears as tasty as a well-barbecued roadkill dinner: *courage*. Now, I know what you're thinking: "Courage? Isn't that just for superheroes and folks who voluntarily eat habanero peppers?" Courage is the main ingredient in your recipe for conquering life's toughest challenges. You see, courage isn't about not feeling fear. It's about looking fear straight in its beady little possum eyes and saying, "Nice try, buddy, but I've got a barbecue to attend." It's that gut-churning, heart-pounding moment when you decide to take action despite every fiber of your being screaming, "Run away! Hide! Play dead like a possum!"

Courage is essential for facing difficult tasks, because it's the bridge between your comfort zone and your "I can't believe I just did that" zone. It's what transforms, "I can't," into, "I did." Without courage, we'd all be stuck in our cozy little burrows, never tasting the sweet (or savory) flavor of victory.

Now, let's talk about risk-taking. Courage and risk-taking go together like possums and trash cans. Every time you summon the courage to face a challenge, you're taking a risk. You might fail, you might look silly, you might end up with barbecue sauce all over your face. But here's the kicker: without taking risks, you'll never grow. It's like trying to become a master chef by only ever eating microwave dinners. It's like walking in ankle deep water pretending to swim. Sure, it's safe, but where's the fun in that? Personal growth is the prize at the end of your courage-fueled journey. Each time you face a fear or overcome a challenge; you're adding another notch to your possum-eating belt. You're becoming stronger, more resilient, and more confident. Before you know it, you'll be looking at challenges that used to terrify you and thinking, *huh, that looks about as scary as a sleeping possum.*

Just remember this: courage isn't about being fearless. It's about being scared out of your wits, but deciding to take action, anyway. It's about taking risks, embracing the possibility of failure, and knowing that even if you fall flat on your face, you'll get up with a great story to tell (and maybe a few possum teeth marks to show off).

DIFFERENT TYPES OF COURAGE

Just like there's more than one way to barbecue a possum, there's more than one type of courage you'll need to face life's toughest challenges. Physical courage is what most folks think of first: it's the guts to stare down a hissing possum or climb that rickety ladder to clean your gutters. But let me tell you, sometimes the scariest possums aren't the ones with sharp teeth and beady eyes. Sometimes they're the ones lurking in your own mind. That's where emotional courage comes in handy. It's the strength to face those feelings you've been stuffing down deeper than a possum in a trash can. Maybe it's finally having that tough conversation with your spouse or admitting you need help with an addiction. It ain't easy, but neither is prying a possum off your porch.

Then there's moral courage: standing up for what's right even when everyone else is telling you to sit down and shut up. It might mean being the only one at the church potluck who refuses to laugh at an unkind joke or speaking up when you see someone being mistreated at work. And don't forget intellectual courage: that's the willingness to challenge your own ideas and learn new things, even if it means admitting you were wrong. It's like trying a new possum recipe when you've been cooking it the same way for years. Each type of courage is like a different tool in your possum-eating toolkit. Sometimes you need a big knife to tackle the tough bits, and other times you need a delicate touch to pick out the bones. The key is knowing which type of courage to use when life serves up its next platter of challenges.

How about exercising your courage to eat the possum?

THE POSSUM-SIZED COURAGE CHALLENGE

Maybe you are like other people and need help to build your courage muscle gradually, preparing you to face your biggest "possum" (challenge) with confidence. Remember: just like eating a possum, tackling your fears is best done one bite at a time! So, here is an exercise to help you build your courage:

STEP 1: IDENTIFY A POSSUM

Write down your biggest challenge or fear: your "possum." It doesn't necessarily have to be *the* possum, but something that you want to overcome that has been difficult. Be specific about what scares you and why.

Step 2: Break It Down

Divide your "possum" into smaller, more manageable pieces. List 5-10 smaller actions that lead up to facing your big challenge.

Step 3: Create Your Courage Ladder

Arrange these smaller actions from least scary to most scary. This is your Courage Ladder. It might be helpful to make one (or use the one in the *Eat the Possum Journal*).

Step 4: Start Climbing

Begin with the least scary action on your ladder. Give yourself a deadline to complete it within the next week.

Step 5: Reflect and Celebrate

After completing each step, write down:

- How you felt before, during, and after
- What you learned
- How you can apply this to the next step

Celebrate each small victory with a possum-themed reward (e.g., treat yourself to some barbecue).

STEP 6: KEEP CLIMBING

Move to the next rung on your Courage Ladder. Repeat steps 4-5 for each level.

STEP 7: FACE YOUR POSSUM

When you reach the top of your ladder, it's time to face your big "possum." Use the confidence and skills you've built to take on your challenge.
Bonus: Possum Pep Talk
Before each step, give yourself a "Possum Pep Talk." Say out loud: "I've eaten smaller possums before, and I can eat this one too!"
Remember, building courage is like barbecuing a possum—it takes time, patience, and a willingness to try something new. Keep at it, and soon you'll be feasting on success!
But what if you are scared?
Now, let's talk about fear: that slimy, hissing critter that's been keeping you from sinking your teeth into life's juiciest challenges. We all know fear; it's that voice in your head saying, "Whoa there, partner! That possum looks mighty scary. Maybe we should just stick to our usual diet of safe, boring salads." But here's the thing: if you want to taste the sweet barbecue sauce of success, you've got to learn to stare that fear-possum right in its beady little eyes.
I'm not saying fear is all bad. Sometimes it's there to keep us from doing something truly stupid, like trying to pet a rabid

raccoon or investing our life savings in a pyramid scheme involving magic beans. But more often than not, fear is just a big bully, trying to keep us trapped in our comfort zones. And let me tell you, comfort zones are about as exciting as a possum-free picnic. So how do we overcome this fear and build up our courage muscles? Well, grab your metaphorical barbecue tongs, because we're about to dig into some juicy strategies.

1. Name that possum: First things first, you've got to identify what you're afraid of: Is it a failure? Rejection? Looking silly in front of others? Write it down, say it out loud, and sing it if you want to. The point is, once you've named your fear, it loses some of its power. It's like turning on the light and realizing that scary monster in your closet is just a pile of laundry you've been avoiding.
2. Break it down into bite-sized pieces: Eating a whole possum in one go might seem overwhelming, but what about taking just one small bite? The same goes for facing your fears. Break that big, scary goal into smaller, more manageable steps. Want to start a business? Maybe start by researching your market or creating a simple business plan. Before you know it, you'll have eaten that whole fear-possum, one bite at a time.
3. Visualize your victory: Close your eyes and imagine yourself conquering that fear. See yourself giving that presentation with confidence, asking that person out on a date, or whatever your personal possum might be. The more vividly you can picture your success, the more your brain will believe it's possible. It's like mental barbecue sauce, making that fear-possum more palatable.
4. Practice the "What's the worst that could happen?" game: Often, our fears are way worse in our heads

than in reality. So, play this game: Ask yourself, "What's the worst that could happen if I face this fear?" Then, follow up with, "And how would I handle that?" You might find that even the worst-case scenario isn't as bad as you thought, and you're more capable of handling it than you realized.
5. Surround yourself with possum-eaters: find people who inspire you, who've faced their fears, and come out victorious. Their courage can be contagious. Plus, they might have some great tips on the best barbecue sauce for fear-possums.

Remember, overcoming fear isn't about being fearless. It's about feeling the fear and doing it, anyway. It's about looking at that possum on your plate and saying, "You know what? I'm going to take a bite, even if my knees are shaking and my stomach's doing somersaults."

Facing down the hardest things in your life puts you in rarified air, for others have also faced overwhelming challenges and are thriving despite the opposition. Here are a few of their stories.

1. JONI EARECKSON TADA

At age seventeen, Joni became a quadriplegic after a diving accident. Despite her paralysis, she learned to paint with her mouth and became an internationally known mouth artist. She founded Joni and Friends, a global ministry serving people with disabilities. For over fifty years, Joni has been a powerful advocate, author and speaker, sharing her faith journey of finding purpose and joy despite her physical limitations. She has written over fifty books and received numerous awards for her advocacy work.

2. NICK VUJICIC

Born without limbs due to a rare disorder, Nick faced bullying and depression as a child. Through his faith, he overcame suicidal thoughts and found purpose in inspiring others. He became a motivational speaker, author, and founder of the nonprofit Life Without Limbs. Nick has spoken to millions worldwide about overcoming adversity through faith. He is married with four children and continues to inspire people globally with his message of hope.

3. GRACIA BURNHAM

Gracia and her husband Martin were missionaries in the Philippines when they were kidnapped by terrorists in 2001 and held hostage in the jungle for over a year. Martin was killed during a rescue attempt, but Gracia survived. Despite her trauma, she forgave her captors and continues to share her story of faith under extreme circumstances. She established the Martin and Gracia Burnham Foundation to support missionary work. Gracia speaks about her experiences and has written two books on finding God's grace in the midst of terror.

These modern-day examples demonstrate how faith can enable ordinary people to respond to extraordinary challenges with remarkable courage, forgiveness and perseverance. Their stories continue to inspire many.

There's more about fear that you need to know!

Let's talk about why your brain goes into full-on panic mode when you spot a hissing, beady-eyed critter in your trash can. Our brains have a hair-trigger fear response; it is a "shoot first, ask questions later" approach to potential threats. It's like your brain has an overactive security system, setting off blaring alarms at the slightest rustle in the bushes. Better to have a few false alarms than miss the one time it's actually a hungry predator, right?

But here's the kicker: our brains haven't quite caught up to the fact that we're more likely to be taken out by a texting driver than a mountain lion these days. So, we're left with an alarm system that goes bonkers over things that aren't actually that dangerous. Possums, public speaking, asking for a raise—you name it, our brains are ready to label it as a life-or-death situation. It's like having a super-sensitive smoke detector that goes off every time you make toast. Sure, it might save your life in a real fire, but most of the time, it's just making you jump out of your skin for no good reason. So next time you find yourself face-to-face with a "terrifying" possum, remember: your brain is just trying to keep you alive, even if it's being a bit dramatic about it.

Now, let's talk about the fear-courage seesaw. Imagine a playground seesaw. On one end, we've got fear: that voice in your head saying, "Nope, nope, nope!" On the other end, there's courage: the part of you ready to wrestle that possum with your bare hands (which, by the way, we don't recommend). The trick is finding the right balance, so you're not stuck on either extreme. Too much fear, and you'll miss out on life's adventures. You'll be the person who never tries new foods, never takes that dream vacation, and definitely never eats the possum. But too much courage without any fear? That's a recipe for disaster. You'll be the guy poking a sleeping bear with a stick, thinking, *what could go wrong?* Or screaming, "Watch this!" to your wife as you singe your eyebrows off by doing something stupid. The sweet spot is right in the middle—where you've got enough fear to keep you from doing anything truly stupid but enough courage to push past your comfort zone and grow. It's about acknowledging your fear, giving it a little nod of appreciation for trying to keep you safe, and then gently pushing past it when it's holding you back unnecessarily. Remember, the goal isn't to eliminate fear entirely; it's to develop a more balanced response so you can face life's challenges (and possums) with confidence.

So, how does your specific personality type approach

courage? This is vital if you are to leverage the way God wired you in order for you to experience successfully devouring every last morsel of the delicious possum barbecue.

ANALYTICAL ALEX (THINKER):

Approach to Courage: Analytical Alex tends to approach courage through careful planning and risk assessment. He gathers information, analyzes potential outcomes, and creates strategies before taking action.

Leveraging Strengths: Use your analytical skills to break down your fears into manageable components. Create a detailed plan of action, considering all possible scenarios.

Biblical Example: The apostle Paul's methodical approach to spreading the gospel, even in the face of persecution, demonstrates this type of courage.

PRINCIPLED PAULA (PERSISTER):

Approach to Courage: Principled Paula's courage stems from her strong moral convictions. She's willing to stand firm in her beliefs, even when facing opposition.

Leveraging Strengths: Align your courageous actions with your core values. When facing a challenge, remind yourself of the principles you're upholding.

Biblical Example: Daniel's unwavering faith in the face of the lion's den exemplifies this courage rooted in principles.

EMPATHETIC EMMA (HARMONIZER):

Approach to Courage: Empathetic Emma finds courage in supporting and standing up for others. Her bravery often manifests in acts of compassion and selflessness.

Leveraging Strengths: Frame your courageous actions in terms of how they'll benefit or support others. This can provide additional motivation.

Biblical Example: Mary, the mother of Jesus, showed great courage in accepting her role, motivated by her care for others and obedience to God.

CHARISMATIC CHARLIE (PROMOTER):

Approach to Courage: Charismatic Charlie's courage is often spontaneous and fueled by enthusiasm. He's willing to take risks and try new things without overthinking.

Leveraging Strengths: Use your natural enthusiasm to push past fear. Your ability to inspire others can also help you gather support for courageous endeavors.

Biblical Example: Peter's bold declaration of Jesus as the Messiah shows this type of spontaneous courage.

SPONTANEOUS SAM (REBEL):

Approach to Courage: Spontaneous Sam's courage often manifests as a willingness to challenge the status quo. He's not afraid to be different or go against conventional wisdom.

Leveraging Strengths: Embrace your rebellious nature as a source of courage. Reframe fear as an opportunity to prove others wrong or break new ground.

Biblical Example: Samson's unconventional methods of fighting the Philistines demonstrate this type of courage.

CONTEMPLATIVE CORY (IMAGINER):

Approach to Courage: Contemplative Cory finds courage through visualization and imagination. He can envision positive outcomes, which helps him face his fears.

Leveraging Strengths: Use your rich inner world to visualize success. Create detailed mental images of yourself overcoming your fears.

Biblical Example: John's vivid visions in Revelation show how imagination can fuel courage in the face of adversity.

AMBITIOUS AVA (ACHIEVER):

Approach to Courage: Ambitious Ava's courage is often goal oriented. She's willing to face fears if it means achieving her objectives.

Leveraging Strengths: Set clear, ambitious goals related to overcoming your fears. Use your drive for achievement to push past obstacles.

Biblical Example: Nehemiah's courageous leadership in rebuilding Jerusalem's walls demonstrates this goal-oriented bravery.

INTUITIVE IAN (DISCERNER):

Approach to Courage: Intuitive Ian (Discerner)'s courage comes from trusting their gut feelings. He's willing to take leaps of faith based on his intuition.

Leveraging Strengths: Learn to trust your intuition when facing fears. Your ability to sense patterns can help you navigate uncertain situations.

Biblical Example: The prophet Jeremiah's willingness to

deliver unpopular messages based on his spiritual intuition shows this type of courage.

ADVENTUROUS ANDY (EXPLORER):

Approach to Courage: Adventurous Andy sees courage as an exciting challenge. He's naturally inclined to step out of his comfort zone and try new things.

Leveraging Strengths: Frame your fears as exciting new territories to explore. Your natural curiosity can help overcome hesitation.

Biblical Example: Abraham's willingness to leave his homeland for an unknown destination exemplifies this adventurous courage.

CAUTIOUS CATHY (QUESTIONER):

Approach to Courage: Cautious Cathy's courage comes from thorough understanding. She faces her fears by gathering information and asking questions until she feels prepared.

Leveraging Strengths: Use your questioning nature to understand your fears better. The more you know, the more confident you'll feel in facing them.

Biblical Example: Thomas's courage to voice his doubts and seek evidence of Jesus' resurrection demonstrates this questioning approach to bravery.

We have included biblical examples of individuals in the personality types, but the many stories of courage in Scripture are awe-inspiring. Throughout the Bible, courage is portrayed as a vital attribute for those who follow God. One of the most prominent examples is found in the book of Joshua, where God repeatedly exhorts Joshua to "Be strong and courageous" (1:6-9). This command wasn't just about physical bravery but about having the spiritual fortitude to lead God's people and trust in His promises. We see similar encouragement in Deuteronomy 31:6, where Moses tells the Israelites, "Be strong and courageous. Do not be afraid or terrified because of them, for the Lord your God goes with you; he will never leave you nor forsake you." These passages emphasize that biblical courage is rooted in faith and trust in God's presence and promises, rather than in one's own strength.

The Bible is filled with stories of individuals displaying remarkable courage in the face of adversity. David, a young shepherd, courageously faced the giant Goliath, declaring, "The Lord who rescued me from the paw of the lion and the paw of the bear will rescue me from the hand of this Philistine" (1 Samuel 17:37). Esther risked her life to save her people, famously stating, "If I perish, I perish" (Esther 4:16). Daniel continued to pray openly to God despite the threat of being thrown into a den of lions (Daniel 6). In the New Testament, we see the apostles boldly proclaiming the gospel despite persecution, with Peter and John asserting, "We cannot help speaking about what we have seen and heard" (Acts 4:20). These examples illustrate that biblical courage often involves standing firm in one's faith and doing what is right, even in the face of danger or opposition, trusting that God is in control.

Remember, possum eaters, your unique personality is not a barrier to courage—it's your secret sauce! By understanding your "you" factor, you can tailor your approach to courage in a way that feels authentic and leverages your natural strengths. Whether you're an Analytical Alex meticulously planning your possum-eating strategy or a Spontaneous Sam ready to take a bite without hesitation, your personality can be your greatest ally in facing your fears. So, embrace your unique traits, and let's show those possums who's boss!

Now it's time to flex those courage muscles in your everyday life. You see, courage isn't just about facing down grizzly bears or jumping out of airplanes (though if that's your thing, more power to you). It's about those small, daily acts of bravery that most folks overlook. It's choosing to speak up in a meeting when you've got a different opinion, trying that new recipe even though you've burned water before, or striking up a conversation with that neighbor you've been avoiding for months. These might seem like small potatoes compared to eating a possum, but here's the secret: each of these little acts of courage is like doing a rep at the bravery gym. You're building up your courage muscles, bit by bit, day by day. And before you know it, when that big, scary possum of a challenge comes lumbering into your life, you'll be ready to face it head-on, armed with the strength you've built up from all those "minor" acts of courage.

Now, let's chew on what happens after you've taken that brave bite of possum. Sure, it might taste a bit funky at first, but here's the thing: the aftertaste of courage is sweeter than you could ever imagine. Each time you face a fear, whether it's a tiny mouse of a challenge or a full-grown possum, you're not just overcoming that specific obstacle. You're growing as a person, expanding your comfort zone, and proving to yourself that you're capable of more than you ever thought possible. It's like adding another notch to your possum-eating belt. And the best part? This personal growth snowballs. The more courageous acts you stack up, the more confident you become, and the more willing you are to take on even bigger challenges. So, my fellow possum eaters, remember this: every act of courage, no matter how small, is a step towards becoming the bravest, most possum-eating version of yourself. Now, who's ready to go find their next possum?

A SUMMARY OF CHAPTER 2 OF *EAT THE POSSUM*:

1. Courage is essential for facing life's toughest challenges.
2. Courage isn't about being fearless, but about taking action despite fear.
3. Different types of courage exist: physical, emotional, moral, and intellectual.
4. The Possum-Sized Courage Challenge offers a step-by-step approach to building courage.
5. Overcoming fear involves strategies like naming fears, breaking challenges into smaller steps, and visualization.
6. Our brains have an overactive fear response that often exaggerates perceived threats.
7. The goal is to find a balance on the "fear-courage seesaw."
8. Different personality types approach courage in unique ways.
9. Biblical examples illustrate various forms of courage.
10. Courage in daily life involves small acts of bravery that build "courage muscles."
11. Facing fears leads to personal growth and increased confidence.
12. The chapter includes inspiring stories of individuals who overcame significant challenges.
13. Understanding your personality type can help leverage your strengths in facing fears.
14. The "you" factor emphasizes that individual traits can be assets in developing courage.
15. Courage often involves trusting in God's promises and standing firm in faith.
16. The aftermath of courageous acts leads to expanded comfort zones and personal development.

17. Surrounding yourself with supportive people can help in building courage.
18. The chapter encourages readers to embrace their unique traits in facing challenges.
19. Courage is portrayed as a skill that can be developed over time with practice.
20. The overall message emphasizes that everyone is capable of facing their "possums" with the right approach and mindset.

QUESTIONS TO HELP YOU GROW

1. How does the author's comparison of courage to "barbecuing a possum" help illustrate the concept? What insights does this metaphor provide about facing life's challenges?
2. The chapter discusses different types of courage (physical, emotional, moral, and intellectual). Which type do you find most challenging personally, and why?
3. How might understanding your specific personality type (as described in the chapter) help you approach courage in a way that feels more authentic to you?
4. The author suggests that small, daily acts of bravery can build "courage muscles." What are some small courageous acts you could incorporate into your daily life?
5. Reflect on the biblical examples of courage mentioned in the chapter. How do these stories relate to modern-day challenges, and what lessons can we draw from them?
6. The chapter discusses the balance between fear and courage. How can you distinguish between healthy caution and paralyzing fear in your own life?

7. The author states, "The aftertaste of courage is sweeter than you could ever imagine." Recall a time when you acted courageously. How did it impact your personal growth and confidence?

CHAPTER THREE
SNIFFING OUT YOUR PERSONAL POSSUM

P ossums are literally everywhere! They hide in stumps, haystacks, vine tangles, attics, garages, road ditches, hollow trees, rock piles, crannies, under buildings, and abandoned burrows of other animals. They are everywhere, and they don't hibernate. They are likely near you, ready to invade your local trash can, but you cannot see them.

Even though you have identified your possum, the perceived problem may not be the real problem.

Like possums, hard things in your life are likely hiding in plain sight. They may be in stealth mode, occupying a blind spot in your life. You may be stepping over, going around, or treating it like the elephant in the room by ignoring it. Even worse, it may camouflage itself so well that you spend your life treating the symptoms of the hard thing instead of addressing the real cause of your problem. For example, the tricky thing in a relationship may not be that the people have drifted apart; it may be due to another entity that has robbed them of their emotional connection. It may be a job, an emotional affair, or indifference to one another.

Someone once said, "The problem with most problems is that the problem is not really the problem." If that's the case, your hard thing may be a symptom of something larger. Treating the symptoms without treating the actual *cause of the problem* will be an endless game of your hard thing playing possum. When you think you have conquered it, it comes alive and waddles into another place in your life.

That's why a little deeper view of the problem is necessary. You might have already identified your possum, but you also need to know if the possum is the cause, or simply a symptom of something deeper.

How do you determine the root cause of a problem?

Jennifer Haury suggests brainstorming first, where you include everything and everyone involved in the hard thing you want to overcome.[1] For example, if your problem is spending too much money, you look at who is creating the issue and what is causing it. It may be that the budget is unrealistic, or that someone is overspending. It may not be a people problem, but a paper (budget) problem. Be careful not to personalize the problem; in other words, make the person the problem. Doing so may hinder success because you blame the person instead of seeking ways to overcome the issue.

Haury suggests asking, "Why?" five times, which is a form of "Root Cause Analysis," a modern psychological tool to determine the root cause of a problem.

Here's an example of using the "Five Whys" technique to analyze why a person is finding it hard to lose weight.

Problem statement: I find it hard to lose weight.

1. Why? I'm not seeing results despite trying to eat healthier and exercise.
2. Why? I often end up overeating, especially in the evenings.

---

[1]. Jennifer Haury, "Easy Problem Solving Using the 4-step Method," MRSC Insight (blog), June 7, 2017.
https://mrsc.org/stay-informed/mrsc-insight/june-2017/4-step-problem-solving-method

3. Why? I feel stressed and tired after work, which leads to emotional eating.
4. Why? My job is demanding, and I'm not getting enough sleep.
5. Why? I'm working long hours and bringing work stress home with me.

Root Cause: The underlying issue appears to be work-related stress and poor work-life balance, which is affecting sleep patterns and leading to emotional eating.

This analysis reveals that the difficulty in losing weight isn't simply about diet and exercise, but rather stems from deeper issues related to work stress, sleep, and emotional well-being. Addressing these root causes could potentially lead to more effective weight loss efforts.

To validate this root cause, we could ask: If the person were able to reduce work stress, improve their work-life balance, and get better sleep, would it likely prevent the overeating and make weight loss easier? If the answer is yes, then we've likely identified a significant root cause.

Potential solutions based on this analysis might include:

1. Implementing stress management techniques such as prayer, meditating on Scripture, exercise, etc.
2. Setting boundaries between work and personal life.
3. Improving sleep hygiene.
4. Developing healthier coping mechanisms for stress.
5. Considering a job change or discussing workload with supervisors.

The Five Whys are something used in root cause analysis and can be used in a variety of settings to determine the root cause of a problem. For example, if a car does not start, the root cause may be a faulty starter, engine failure, dead battery, or the vehicle is out of fuel. If that is the case, then you would write all the possible reasons for the problem and begin determining which situation is the reason for the issue.

However, if the problem is a strained relationship, it may require revisiting the event where the strain occurred. This is a "where or when" place where you look at the event's origin. Determining the reason for the strain may not be as easy as it seemed at the point of strain, so an honest look at the event may shed light on the root cause of the problem. A trusted friend, counselor, or pastor may help you walk through this process and determine what caused the issue in the first place.

Finding the root cause requires looking at who and what, then when or where it occurred. The next step is understanding why.

If you know why, then it is best to ask, "Why?" five times, or until it no longer makes sense to ask, "Why?" If you are unsure why it occurred, then brainstorming may help you determine possible reasons why. At this point, one or two areas should become clear.

Here is a Possum Identification Worksheet. It is also found in the Workbook and Possum Journal:

STEP 1: BRAINSTORMING

List all the challenges or obstacles you're currently facing in your life:

1. _____
2. _____
3. _____
4. _____
5. _____

STEP 2: THE FIVE WHYS ANALYSIS

Choose the most pressing challenge from your list and apply the Five Whys technique:

Challenge: _____

1. Why is this a challenge? _____
2. Why? _____
3. Why? _____
4. Why? _____
5. Why? _____

Root Cause: _____

STEP 3: IDENTIFY INVOLVED PARTIES

Who is involved in or affected by this challenge?

1. _____
2. _____
3. _____

STEP 4: DETERMINE THE ORIGIN

When or where did this challenge first occur?

_____

STEP 5: UNDERSTAND THE "WHY"

Why is overcoming this challenge important to you?

_____

STEP 6: HIDDEN ASPECTS

Are there any hidden aspects or "secret possums" related to this challenge?

1. _____
2. _____
3. _____

STEP 7: POTENTIAL SOLUTIONS

List possible ways to address this challenge:

1. _____
2. _____
3. _____

STEP 8: OBSTACLES TO OVERCOME

What obstacles might prevent you from addressing this challenge?

1. _____
2. _____
3. _____

STEP 9: SUPPORT SYSTEM

Who can support you in overcoming this challenge?

1. _____
2. _____
3. _____

STEP 10: POSSUM DECLARATION

Based on this analysis, my "possum" (the most challenging thing I need to overcome) is:

_____

Remember, identifying your "possum" is the first step towards overcoming it. Be honest with yourself throughout this process and don't hesitate to seek help from trusted friends or mentors if needed.

Your possum may be more apparent than this, however.

You must identify the possum and the root cause of your hard thing if you are to truly eat the possum, because your efforts to rid your life of it will reveal other "animals," rather than the one you need to overcome.

Some struggle with the "Why" questioning. Is it biblical to ask, 'Why'?

Is asking why five times biblical? While the Five Whys technique is a modern problem-solving method, there are several instances in the Bible where characters engaged in a similar process of questioning to get to the root of an issue. Moses repeatedly questioned God about his mission to lead the Israelites out of Egypt, asking "Why me?" and "What if they don't believe me?" This series of questions helped Moses understand the root of his calling and God's plan (Exodus 3:1-14). Throughout the book of Job, Job repeatedly asks, "Why?" regarding his suffering, seeking to understand the root cause of his misfortunes. In Judges 6:11-24, Gideon questions the angel about why Israel is suffering under Midianite oppression, seeking to understand the root cause of their troubles. In Mark 10:17-22, Jesus uses a series of questions to help the rich young ruler understand the root of his spiritual condition and what's holding him back from true discipleship.

In their conversation in John 3:1-21, Nicodemus asks Jesus

several questions, seeking to understand the concept of being "born again" and the root of spiritual rebirth. And, finally, on the road to Emmaus, Jesus asks the disciples a series of questions to help them understand why they were downcast and to reveal the root of their misunderstanding about His death and resurrection (Luke 24:13-35).

While these examples don't follow the exact Five Whys format, they do demonstrate a similar process of questioning to uncover deeper truths or root causes.

AUNT NELLIE

My great Aunt Nellie was the kind of woman who would give us a nickel from her band-aid box in the refrigerator, a drink of ice-cold milk with cookies, or fresh muscadine grapes from her grapevine behind her house each time we visited her. For those reasons, we stopped at her house often.

Once, another great aunt (Aunt Shirley) from Atlanta, Georgia, visited us in North Little Rock, Arkansas. My younger brother began to piece together the family connections as she talked with the family, learning that they were sisters-in-law. He was overjoyed and asked Aunt Shirley, "So your brother was Uncle John, Aunt Nellie's husband?"

She replied, "Yes, we are related by marriage."

He said, "That's incredible. We should see Aunt Nellie right now. She is home, and her door is open."

My brother did not know that when my uncle John died, Aunt Shirley believed that Aunt Nellie did not do enough to save his life. He died of cancer, and the final days were tough. At John's funeral, Aunt Shirley accused Aunt Nellie of killing her brother. They did not speak for over twenty years. So, my brother's suggestion that Aunt Shirley visit her sister-in-law was the last thing she wanted to do.

When my brother insisted they visit Nellie, Aunt Shirley

made excuses. "Jerry, you know I don't have time to visit. I need to get on the road."

Not knowing their history, he said, "It's no problem. Aunt Nellie lives a few doors away from us, and it will only take a few minutes."

She protested, "I can't go, Jerry. I don't feel good."

Without warning, he walked over to the couch, took her by the hand, pulled her to her feet, and started toward the front door, holding tightly to her hand. All along the way, she tried refusing, but he held tightly to her hand and pulled her all the way to Aunt Nellie's house. I am sure that her high heels left an imprint inches deep in our dirt driveway. All along the way, she tried digging her heels into the gravel road to establish an anchor point. I am sure all of our neighbors heard her protests and opposition to this meeting. My brother kept pulling, though, and eventually they arrived at Aunt Nellie's front door.

The last place Aunt Shirley had ever wanted to be was at her sister-in-law's door. But today was different.

Several things had happened that morning. First, Aunt Nellie woke up thinking about Aunt Shirley, not knowing she was coming for a visit a few doors away. Next, she also felt a strong urge to pray for the restoration of their relationship. She had been wounded and did not want to be hurt again by another string of accusations. But she obeyed the prompting of the Holy Spirit and prayed.

When my brother arrived at Aunt Nellie's door, still holding Aunt Shirley's hand with a death grip, he knocked and announced his presence. Aunt Nellie had severe glaucoma and could not see well at all. She got up from her rocking chair, went to the screen door, and opened it. Jerry stepped out of the way and said, "Look who I brought to see you," revealing Aunt Shirley. In one moment, face to face with the most challenging things, two women reconciled with tears and prayer. It was the most fantastic moment. Just a few months later, Aunt Nellie died. Aunt Shirley died ten years later.

During her prayer time that morning, Aunt Nellie had to determine the root cause of the initial accusations. Her sister-in-law did not honestly believe that Aunt Nellie had killed Uncle John. She was so hurt by losing her brother that her grief found an unhealthy and unfortunate focal point. During her prayer time, Aunt Nellie finally realized that the root problem had nothing to do with her, but instead with something no one could control. She had to release the hurt to God and pray that Aunt Shirley could do the same.

Sometimes, the search for the problem is not what it seems. It is just that we focus on one aspect of the issue or believe that we have identified the culprit when the legitimate problem continues to bring misdirects.

For these aunts, the problem was not only a misdirect from grief but a legitimate need for reconciliation. It should be solution-oriented once we identify the "possum" or the problem.

Revisiting pain from the past without a desire for healing and identifying the healing points of the problem will leave us with deeper wounds than before.

In the case of forgiveness, this is especially true. When a person begins the path of forgiveness, they believe there must be a meeting of the minds with the one that offended them for forgiveness to blossom. They erroneously think they are supposed to confront the person, proceed with the evidence of the offense, and declare forgiveness to the person who hurt them. There are times when this process is necessary, but one must realize that such a venture may not bring about closure to the offense as intended. In fact, it may cause more significant pain than the original problem.

For example, in Aunt Shirley and Aunt Nellie's situation, if Aunt Nellie had gone to Aunt Shirley immediately after Uncle John's death and shared the hurt that Shirley created by her accusation, my aunt may have said, "I don't care what you say, you killed my brother," driving the wound even deeper.

The one forgiving may not receive the validation of the

offense from the offender. Instead, they may be oblivious to the wound or intentionally drive it deeper because of their pain. The expected result may significantly differ from the outcome. In these cases, it may force the wound deeper instead of leading to reconciliation. While eating a possum may require steps to reconciliation, unless one understands the nature or cause of the wound, they will continue to fail in their attempts to eat the possum, only dealing with the symptoms of the problem. This is not a recipe for success, but may debilitate future attempts to overcome the issue.

Successfully overcoming the obstacle or, in our case, "eating the possum" requires identifying the real issue, not a symptom of it. You may also need another person to help you determine the root cause. It may hide in plain sight, but we easily overlook what we should see. Who you surround yourself with will determine the level of success you experience.

But there is a warning I must share: Overcoming your hard thing will *never* take you contrary to Scripture. It will align with Scripture and the heart of God. Just because you face a *hard thing* does not mean the solution is what you think it is. In other words, this is *not* an excuse to wreck your family or life because something is too hard, nor a reason to steer clear of hard things to the detriment of your family. Sometimes people look for an easy way out and choose the most convenient one because every way out is hard. If working through a marriage issue is complicated, an equally hard thing to do is to divorce and find someone else. Unfortunately, you will not find the victory you seek because you stepped out of God's plan. I have witnessed people excusing a decision that was catastrophic to their family, job, or whatever to do "the hard thing" when it did not require that.

That is the flip side of overcoming. We might think that overcoming an issue requires great difficulty when, in reality, it is somewhat easy.

We can't make overcoming harder to do than it really is.

An example of this is a father I once talked to about

attending a Christian university to train to be a minister. He was working at an RV manufacturing company, making a good living for his family, when God called him to ministry. I encouraged him to attend the university online *while* maintaining his job and supporting his family. I had experienced the same journey and found success in my educational pursuit while continuing to work. He felt God was calling him to do the hard thing, but misunderstood the nature of God's call. It *was* to attend the seminary. He took it to mean he was to do something catastrophic, and, unfortunately, it was. He moved to Minnesota with his family, his money ran out, and he and his family ended up homeless in the winter with two kids under four years of age. They eventually landed at a campground, living in a tent, in the winter.

Sometimes, we make the hard thing a *lot* harder than it should be, so be careful not to create a catastrophic situation in your attempt to obey God's leading. Eating a possum does not have to be destructive, but people can be overdramatic. Ask anyone at that barbecue if a particular pastor was being overdramatic. I am sure they will agree that such a foray into the culinary delight of eating possum does not require a catastrophic consequence from the pastor. Neither does your hard thing. It may be challenging, but one should be aware that it is not disastrous.

Correctly identifying your possum is the first step, but if you have a difficult time identifying the problem, trusted friends may be able to help you discover the hidden possums that seek to wreck your pantry. This leads us to the next step: Once you correctly identify the possum, you are ready to surround yourself with the right individuals.

IDENTIFY YOUR POSSUM QUESTIONS

1. After completing the Possum Identification Worksheet, what surprised you most about your identified "possum"? How has this exercise changed your understanding of your challenge?
2. How might the Five Whys technique help you uncover hidden aspects of your challenges that you hadn't considered before?
3. Reflect on the story of Aunt Nellie and Aunt Shirley. How might identifying the root cause of a problem in your own life lead to unexpected reconciliation or healing?
4. Consider the warning about solutions not being contrary to Scripture. How can you ensure that your approach to overcoming your "possum" aligns with your values and beliefs?
5. How can you apply the concept of solution-oriented thinking to your identified possum? What specific solutions can you brainstorm?

A SUMMARY OF CHAPTER 3 OF *EAT THE POSSUM*:

- Possums, like hard things in life, are often hiding in plain sight.
- The perceived problem may not be the real problem; it could be a symptom of something deeper.
- Identifying the root cause of a problem is crucial for effective problem-solving.
- The Five Whys technique is a useful tool for root cause analysis.
- Personalization of problems should be avoided to prevent hindering success.

- Work-related stress and poor work-life balance can often be underlying causes of seemingly unrelated issues.
- The Possum Identification Worksheet is a helpful tool for identifying and analyzing challenges.
- Asking, "Why?" is biblically supported, as demonstrated by various examples in scripture.
- Reconciliation and forgiveness may require understanding of the root cause of conflicts.
- Overcoming obstacles should align with Scripture and not be used as an excuse for destructive behavior.
- Sometimes we may overcomplicate the process of overcoming challenges.
- Trusted friends can help identify hidden "possums" in our lives.

PRACTICAL APPLICATIONS:

- Use the Possum Identification Worksheet to analyze your challenges.
- Apply the Five Whys technique to uncover root causes of problems.
- Seek support from trusted individuals when identifying and addressing challenges.
- Be cautious not to make overcoming challenges unnecessarily difficult or destructive.
- Ensure that your approach to overcoming obstacles aligns with your values and beliefs.

CHAPTER FOUR

ASSEMBLING YOUR POSSUM-HUNTING POSSE

The people you surround yourself with can encourage peace and success or bring drama and defeat. I have served a faith-based drug and alcohol rehab and have witnessed the effects of the wrong kinds of friends. In many cases, the person with an addiction may not have as much of an addictive behavior at the onset, but may harbor a deep desire to fit in. In those cases, being a part of a group that accepts the person is not always redemptive. It can be catastrophic. Everyone looks for validation and a tribe to belong, but not every tribe is worthy of our participation. It may bring drama and pain, or worse—it may cost us our lives.

On the positive side, surrounding yourself with the right individuals can set you up for great success. Someone once said, "Show me your friends, and I will show you your future." In other words, the people you surround yourself with can make you better than you ever knew or can pull you down. That's why you must be very intentional about who you associate with and why, especially when dealing with a hard thing in your life.

Identifying your problem (or, in our case, possum) requires you to surround yourself with the right people to help you eat your possum. Remember, my buffet at the wild game barbecue included a chorus of individuals who encouraged me to eat the possum. While they were having fun, and I was uncertain of their intention, their goading pushed me to do something I would not have typically done. I can hear the gears in your head working now. Because you are likely saying, "But they were goading you to eat something you didn't want to eat. They were bad for you." While that may seem the case, they proved to be more than fodder for a future book; they encouraged me to face a distasteful problem head-on: tasting a southern delicacy. Cletus was right about the victory over this insignificant, distasteful thing, which could bring success to even more distasteful areas.

Goading and encouragement may be more closely related than you realize; a nagging spouse, for instance, might incessantly urge you to pick yourself up and dust yourself off after being knocked down. They may come across as "nagging," but may serve a more significant function than you know. They may goad you into a great future. It depends on what they are encouraging you to overcome and whether it is genuinely beneficial. If we can suspend a search for ill motives for a moment, sometimes people urge you towards greatness. Sometimes someone goads you into something that may benefit them, but it may also be for your benefit. The people around you may give you the courage to face things you have never encountered, all in the name of goading. Even detractors can serve a purpose of goading you with their disparaging remarks, so that you are energized to success.

Take Michael Jordan's time in high school, for example. Contrary to popular belief, Jordan was not actually cut from his high school varsity team. Rather, as a 5'10" sophomore, he was placed on the junior varsity team to develop his skills further. His high school coach, Clifton "Pop" Herring, made this decision based on Jordan's abilities at the time, noting that while he could handle the ball well, his shooting was only 'merely good,' and his defense was "mediocre." While not totally disparaging, these comments stoked a desire in Michael Jordan to excel in his life, leading him to become arguably one of the greatest basketball players of all time. It mattered how he viewed the comments and what he did with them.

It reminds me of a story by leadership expert Dr. John Maxwell.

He wrote, "When you are trying to realize your dream, sometimes you'll be surprised by which people want to light your fire, and which one's want to put it out." Here's a humorous story he shared to illustrate the point.

A particular migrating bird decided that it was too much trouble to fly south for the winter and decided he would brave the winter out like a lot of other animals do. So, as all the other birds flocked away towards warmer climes, he stayed behind and waited for winter.

By the end of November, he was having serious second thoughts. He had never been so cold and couldn't find any food. Finally, he realized that if he didn't get out of there soon, he wouldn't make it. So, he started to fly south all by himself. After a while, it began to rain. Before he knew it, the water turned to ice on his wings. Struggling, he recognized that he couldn't fly any longer. He knew he was about to die, so he glided down and made his last landing, crashing to the ground in a barnyard.

As he lay there stunned, a cow came by, stepped over him, and dropped a plop right on him. He was totally disgusted. *Here I am*, he thought, *freezing to death. I'm about to die. I'm on my last breath, and then this! What an awful way to go.* So, the bird held his breath and prepared himself to die. But after about two minutes, he discovered that a miracle was happening: He was warming up! The ice on his wings was melting. His muscles were thawing out. His blood was flowing again. He realized that he was going to make it after all. He got so excited and happy that he began to sing a glorious song.

At that moment, the farm's old tomcat was lying in the hayloft in the barn, and he heard the bird singing. He couldn't believe it; he hadn't heard anything like it for months, and he said to himself, *Is that a bird? I thought they'd all gone south for the winter*. He came out of the barn, and lo and behold, there was the bird. The cat crossed over to where he was, pulled him gently out of the cow plop, cleaned him off—and ate him!

There are three morals to this story: (1) Not everyone who drops a plop on you is your enemy; (2) not everyone who takes a plop off you is your friend; and (3) if someone does drop a plop on you, keep your mouth shut.

The same can be said for you as you realize your dream. Some people you consider friends will fight against your success. Others will support you in ways you didn't expect. But no matter which people criticize you or how they do it, don't let them take your focus off your dream.[1]

So how do you determine who will help you overcome the most challenging things in your life? In my experience, four different individuals will help you succeed with your possum.

First, you must enlist the Lord in the battle, and it *will* be a battle. It may be more challenging than you know, and even when you think you have won the fight, you will find that the problem only played dead. Like a possum, it will shuffle off until a more opportune time approaches. Enlisting God in the battle will help you overcome the hard thing, and then you can eat it. God will reveal the source of your struggle, and it may not be what you believe it to be. Scripture tells us that God is an "ever-present help in times of trouble" (Psalm 46:10) and that God encourages us to "call upon the Lord." He will show us unsearchable things (Jeremiah 33:3). Jesus said we could speak to the mountain if we have faith as a mustard seed. Such faith will move the mountain and cast it into the sea (Mark 11:23). Jesus said that while standing on the Mount of Olives with the Dead Sea and the Mediterranean Sea at least twenty miles away. Jesus spoke of faith based on a relationship with God; when you

---

1. Taken from ***The Success Journey*** by John Maxwell. Copyright © 1997 by Maxwell Motivation, Inc., a California Corporation. Used by permission of HarperCollins Christian Publishing. www.harpercollinschristian.com

couple that faith with obedience, all things are possible (Mark 9:23). That does not excuse or diminish the hard things you must overcome, or relieve us of our part in overcoming it, but God's Word informs it. The hard thing is nothing, and God will give you victory over it, but only as you surround yourself with God and obey His leading.

I can't overemphasize your relationship with God enough and the need to obey God no matter how complex your possum may be. If God calls you to overcome it, He will empower you to do it.

Will it be difficult? Absolutely! But victory over it will always require those specific steps of obedience to see the victory. For example, if God leads you to become healthy, he will empower you to become healthy. You must do your part and quit buying sugary snacks and eating to comfort your heart, which is also a great example of identifying your possum. Your biggest problem may not be overeating, but *why* you are overeating. If it is because of an emotional wound or a spiritual hurt, you will need to address the root cause before you begin your health journey, or else it will lead to failure, which will breed further failure. God will help reveal why, but you must heed his call when He does. Most importantly, you must be intentional in doing what you want to do. Too many people believe God to be nothing more than a magician poised for our beck and call, and once summoned, will provide us what we need while we watch and eat Twinkies.

Second, you must have someone that sees the best in you. 1 Samuel 16:1-13 details the prophet Samuel's attempt to find God's next king of Israel. God directed Samuel to the house of Jesse, and Jesse assembled his sons for a sacrifice and to anoint one of them as king. Seven attended, but none met God's criteria for the next king. Even David's father failed to see David as anything more than a shepherd boy, unworthy of being in the presence of a prophet. We don't know if Samuel indicated his true intent before he arrived, but it would be safe to assume that

Jesse would be honored with such a guest and would want all his sons to experience a moment with the prophet of God. Unfortunately, Jesse did not invite David to this great experience. I have always wondered why David was not invited to meet with the prophet. Some believe the reason David was not invited was because he was not a son of Jesse's current wife and the mother of David's brothers (Psalm 51:5), because he was the product of sin; he was an outcast in the family through no fault of his own. Regardless of whether this is correct or not, we know that he was not included in the family meeting with the prophet. Thankfully, God sees more than anyone can and anoints those who meet his criteria rather than those who "fit" the chosen motif.

You will do well to surround yourself with people who see you for what you can become instead of what you have done. Your identity can't be based on a single moment of your life, but on the destiny God desires to establish in you and for you. Finding those who see that in you takes prayer, intentional focus, and God, but please know God wants you to experience that kind of friend.

Look in Scripture, and you will find numerous examples of moments when God saw something that no one else could see in people. David's example is one of many. When Gideon was hiding from the Midianites threshing wheat, the angel of the Lord called him "Mighty Hero." I would have called him the coward of the county or Colonel Chicken. God wrestled with Jacob at the brook and changed his name from deceiver to "prince with God" (Jacob-Israel) right after Jacob fled from Laban in the middle of the night (Genesis 32:28). It could have been the last deceptive practice in Jacob's life, but we don't know for sure. When Jesus called Peter, He called him Peter, or "rock" instead of a "reed" (Peter-Simon), one swaying in the breeze (Matthew 10:2). He did that long before Peter denied the Lord three times (Luke 22:54-62). In each of these occurrences, God did not see them for what they had done or would do in the future, but for who they would become. God sees our purpose before He sees our failure. You do well to find a friend who does the same.

Unfortunately, we listen to those who constantly remind us of our failures; because of that, we feel that we will never amount to anything. That becomes a self-fulfilling prophecy if we heed the examination of our enemies. Honestly, my worst enemy is not outside, but the voice in my head that says that I will never do anything significant or when I can't see anything in me that will ever be more than I am now. That's why I need someone who can see me for who I can become; they can see me better than I or anyone else can see.

If you are going to be the person who can do that hard thing, you have to stop listening to those who don't believe you can do it and enlist the Lord and find that prophetic voice of those around you who see you better, stronger, godlier, and mightier than you see in yourself. Samuel did not see a ruddy young man; he saw a king through prophetic clarity. We need people who see the best in us and call it out. Find one if you do not have such a person in your life. If you can't find them, you will attract them by being that kind of person for those around you. If you can't see the potential because of your personality type, go back to chapter one and find your personality type and the biblical character that closely aligns to that type. You may just be a mighty hero of faith in waiting.

Also, you must surround yourself with someone who will give you spiritual strength. If we were to look at the life of David for such a person, we would see a friend named Jonathan. Jonathan gave David spiritual strength, had his back, and supported him when Jonathan's father (King Saul) sought to kill David (1 Samuel 19). I am amazed at the number of men who do not have a close friend, one who will give them spiritual strength. Jonathan warned David many times about his father's plans, and because of that, David lived. But it was not just that he survived. He *thrived*, because he had someone in his life he could trust. If you have someone in your life that you can trust, you are breathing rarified air, for very few have someone they can trust. Mostly, the most trustworthy people that surround people are their spouses or parents. It is good and healthy if you *at least* have that, but there should also be a neutral third party you can trust. If you don't, become that kind of person to others, and you will naturally draw someone you can trust. Then, cultivate that friendship, and over time, you will begin to see whether that person is a person who gives you spiritual strength or is a drain on your life.

While the person who sees the best in you and gives you spiritual strength may be the same, you also need a neutral third party who can speak truth into your life. David had Nathan. Nathan was a prophet who confronted David with the truth when David sinned with Bathsheba (2 Samuel 12). It would have been easy for David to have had so much pride when confronted with his sin that he could have had Nathan killed just for talking to the king in such a manner. However, David repented. He understood the need to have someone unafraid to point out his sin. There is a significant difference between those who point out your sin based on love and those who are faultfinders ready to exploit your weaknesses. You would be wise to be able to see the difference. There was one, likely closer than Nathan, who would have potentially averted David's disastrous choices, but he said nothing. Joab was such a confidant to David, but there was no record of Joab questioning David's actions. David instructed Joab to place Uriah at the front of the battle and then withdraw from the action (2 Samuel 11:15). Such a move would surely have meant Uriah's death. Maybe fear played a part in the reason Joab said nothing.

Nathan had the same potential threat, but I know fear plays a role in the ability of those who speak into our lives. However, Scripture only records one who spoke up. Only one made a difference. Perhaps their actions would have mitigated the stain on David's character if Joab had counseled King David against his actions with Bathsheba and Uriah. Regardless, David repented and was a man after God's own heart. That was due to a truth speaker in his life, willing to put everything on the line to confront the king.

A truth speaker is vital to your victory over your possum. Why have a truth speaker in your life? If you are like me, you hear too much negative talk about weaknesses and faults coming from between your ears. I often hear condemnation and inadequacy and mostly ignore those voices in my head. But I am thankful to have people around me that I trust who can speak into my life and point out weaknesses that are keeping me from my full potential. It would do you well, too, for there are some things so complicated that they can only be overcome when we are healthy. We must maintain a stance of health if we are to face the formidable enemies around us and in us. The only way to have that kind of health is to address the vulnerabilities that we can't see but that others can help us overcome. A truth speaker will help you adequately address those weak places that the enemy of your soul may exploit.

Do not be discouraged if your current friends are not truth speakers, but toxic people. Instead of speaking life, they act like a clown in a clown car, laughing at your weaknesses, pointing out your failures, and running you down until you are nothing but a heap of frustration.

If that is your current choice of friends, find new ones. Cultivate the kind of friends who can help you win and are not afraid to speak the truth to you. Don't shy away from providing spiritual strength to those around you and don't be too proud to see someone for who they *can be* instead of who they were or are today. Call out their future, lift them, encourage them, and watch for any prideful attempt to exploit their weakness for your gain. Again, if you do not have those kinds of friends, be that kind of friend to others.

How do you find such a supportive network of friends?

When you consider enlisting God in the battle, you have to

be intentional in this by developing a consistent prayer life, asking for God's guidance and strength. You also enlist God through a daily study of Scripture. This will reinforce your faith and understanding of God and provide you with an understanding of developing a life of obedience to God. Finally, ensure you are attending a healthy, Bible-believing church and that you join some type of Bible study group so you can deepen your spiritual connection to other believers and to God.

To find the person who sees the best in you, merely identify those who consistently encourage and believe in you. They are naturally first in line to see who you can be, not just what you have done. Also, actively seek out mentors who have overcome similar challenges to yours. A personal development workshop or seminar that directly relates to your challenge will surround you with like-minded individuals set on eating their own possum.

Third, consider those around you who can provide you with spiritual strength. These are givers who provide you with encouragement for the journey, rather than takers who drain your spiritual strength. Where does one find these spiritual strength givers? Your local, Bible-believing church is a great place to start. Attend faithfully and get to know the people there. Attend the small groups and seek out groups where individuals are also attempting to eat the possum as your challenge.

Finally, identify friends or mentors who are known for their honesty and integrity. Someone who gives constructive feedback in other areas might be a good person to include in this area of your life as you seek out a truth speaker.

Most importantly, become the kind of friend you want to attract. Offer support and encouragement to others who are facing their own challenges. Practice active listening and show empathy to others. Cultivate trust by being reliable and consistent in your interactions with others. Practice vulnerability by sharing your own struggles and successes. Respect others by maintaining confidentiality and boundaries in relationships.

You might have to let go of relationships or diminish exposure to toxic relationships. Rethink your association with those who may not share optimism, which is vital to overcoming your challenge. You are in a battle that requires support on every level, and you can't afford to have around those whose opinion may keep you from victory over your challenge.

If you implement these strategies, you are well on your way to developing great friends and overcoming your possum.

My wife and I are examples of the need to confront the hard things and obey God, even when it does not make sense. We planted a church in Northern Indiana in 2007, and early in 2023, God began lifting the call for that great congregation. We poured our lives into the people and enjoyed ministry to the fullest. The shift came early in the year, and we knew that staying longer than God intended would not benefit the congregation or us. So, we prayed, fasted, sought God, surrounded ourselves with the people who could speak into our hard things and decisions, and then proceeded. The provision of God and the peace of God led us along the way. We saw miraculous things in our transition, including the support of our congregation as we lived what we preached. No significant benefactors supported us, just the gracious hand of God's provision, and we are better off today than we have ever been. I can't take credit for it, for the best support I could ever experience surrounds me. We have those kinds of friends and family members who have encouraged us, provided spiritual strength, spoken truth, and encouraged our obedience to God. You are reading this book because of their actions; each has blessed us. Do not let this frustrate you, though, for if you recognize this need based on what has been written so far, you are further along than you know, and you are preparing yourself for great things ahead. To get there, though, requires you to be the kind of friend you need to someone else. You will save a life, help someone find their destiny, and, in the process, become a magnet for who you want to attract.

Once you have identified your support, you have to do the next step: hurry up!

SURROUND YOURSELF WITH THE RIGHT INDIVIDUALS: QUESTIONS TO HELP YOU GROW

1. Reflecting on the four types of individuals mentioned (God, someone who sees the best in you, someone who gives you spiritual strength, and a truth speaker), who in your life currently fills these roles? Are there any gaps you need to fill?
2. How can you become the kind of friend to others that you need in your own life? What specific actions can you take to cultivate these relationships?
3. Think about a time when someone saw potential in you that you couldn't see yourself. How did this impact your life? How can you cultivate this kind of vision for others?
4. Consider the biblical examples provided (like Samuel seeing David as a king). How can you develop a more prophetic vision for yourself and others?
5. How might your specific personality type (identified in Chapter 1) influence the way you build and maintain supportive relationships? What strengths can you leverage, and what challenges might you need to overcome?

A SUMMARY OF CHAPTER 4 FROM *EAT THE POSSUM*:

- The people you surround yourself with can significantly impact your success or failure in overcoming challenges.
- Four types of individuals are crucial for success:
  1. **God**: Enlist God in your battles through prayer, faith, and obedience.
  2. **Someone who sees the best in you**: Find

people who recognize your potential and encourage your growth.
   3. **Someone who gives you spiritual strength**: Cultivate friendships that provide support and trust.
   4. **A truth speaker**: Seek out individuals who can honestly point out your weaknesses and help you improve.
- Biblical examples illustrate the importance of these relationships (e.g., David and Samuel, David and Jonathan, David and Nathan).
- If you lack these types of supportive relationships, focus on becoming that kind of friend to others.
- Practical steps to build a supportive network:
   1. Develop a consistent prayer life and study Scripture.
   2. Attend a Bible-believing church and join study groups.
   3. Seek out mentors and like-minded individuals.
   4. Participate in personal development workshops.
   5. Practice being a supportive friend to others.
   6. Be willing to let go of toxic relationships that hinder your progress.
   7. Recognize that overcoming challenges ("eating the possum") often requires obedience to God, even when it doesn't make sense.
- Reflect on your current relationships and identify areas where you need more support.
- Consider how your personality type influences your approach to building and maintaining supportive relationships

CHAPTER FIVE

LIGHTING A FIRE UNDER YOUR POSSUM'S TAIL

Once you have surrounded yourself with the right individuals, you are ready to embark on the next phase of eating the possum: HURRY UP! Get a sense of urgency. Light a Fire! DO IT NOW!

Imagine sitting at a plate of heaping Memphis-style barbecue-sauced mystery-flavored meat and letting your mind wander. Mine did, and I wanted to wander off quickly. I could not, and you should not. I could not be paralyzed by overthinking my situation.

Whatever your hard thing is, whether it is possum barbecue or something more insidious, the longer you procrastinate, the easier it is to quit. If it is God's calling, that obedience has a shelf life of about thirty seconds. Let me explain.

Let's say that your possum is your weight and overeating. I am not talking about overeating possums, either. I am talking about just the act of eating. We all do it and need to so our bodies can continue functioning. But not everyone eats because they are hungry. People eat because they are bored, lonely, angry, or hurting. Let's face it: people eat for emotional support, and some even eat because they feel ashamed that they are overweight. It's like a sick carousel where one eats because they are lonely, hurting, sad, and then gain weight, so they eat because they are ashamed that they have gained weight. They become lonelier (because they eat instead of socializing), are hurting, and are sad because they have few friends and continue to gain weight. Rinse and repeat! *That is a sick carousel*! Then, to feel better, they eat more! That person should surround themselves with people who see them as healthy, offer them spiritual strength, and speak the truth, but then what? Being surrounded by the right friends is inadequate if you haven't made their possum-eating urgent.

When individuals commit to making a change, there's a crucial thirty-second window where they must act on their decision to begin the weight loss process. This brief moment of obedience is often the key to turning intentions into actions. In this case, it is *not eating possum* or anything. Well, maybe not *anything*... but eating healthily.

While this is not a weight-loss book (although admittedly, it centers around eating a possum); the principles are the same for weight-loss or doing anything else challenging. We all have a thirty-second window to determine whether we will carry through or procrastinate until we fail. In those thirty seconds, an uncertain smell of barbecued marsupial becomes acute. I must be honest; that was fun to write. But it is true.

The children of Israel faced the Promised Land, and Moses sent twelve spies into the land. They spied the land and returned with a mixed message. The land was truly abundant with "milk and honey," but also with giants and people too numerous to overcome. The people lost heart and threatened to stone Moses and Aaron (Numbers 13-14). The moment was defining, because they were at the hardest place so far, and trusting the Lord was the choice that would open the door to their incredible future. They rebelled and, in their thirty-second window of decision-making, refused to trust God. So, God pronounced judgment: only Joshua and Caleb would step foot in the Promised Land. When the people received the word that God would not let them go in, they tried to repent, but it was too late. They even contemplated going into the Promised Land *without God.* It would be a recipe for disaster. They wandered for forty years because they refused to obey in their thirty-second window.

You have thirty seconds to act once you decide to do something, because you will talk yourself out of change if you don't respond immediately. You will negotiate terms of surrender. You will argue with the devil, your spouse (no, they are not the same), or a trusted friend. You will fail to move, launch, or change. You will list why your situation is too complicated and will never work and become a victim of the inevitable. Your cause will be a self-fulfilling prophecy, because you failed to act in the thirty seconds when God called you to obey. Whatever that aroma from an uncertain smell may be, it will defeat you if you overthink it.

Following are two techniques that may help instill a sense of urgency in your challenges.

Psychologists encourage using the Pomodoro Technique as an exercise to encourage urgency. This time management method uses a timer to break work into intervals, traditionally twenty-five minutes in length, separated by short breaks. Here's how to apply it:

- Choose your possum (task) to tackle
- Set a timer for twenty-five minutes
- Work on the task until the timer rings
- Take a short, five-minute break
- Every four "pomodoros" (twenty-five-minute sessions), take a longer fifteen-to-thirty-minute break

This technique creates urgency by setting a finite time to focus intensely on your task. It also helps prevent burnout by incorporating regular breaks. Eating your possum could mean dedicating focused twenty-five-minute sessions to work on your challenge, creating a sense of immediate action and progress.

Another exercise may help overcome what some might call paralysis by analysis. It is called the 5Second Rule. It was developed by Mel Robbins as a motivation technique that involves counting backward from five to one and then taking immediate physical action. Here's how it works: When you feel the urge to act on a goal, start counting backward: "Five, four, three, two, one." At "One," physically move to take action. You might even say, "*Go*," after, "One." Don't wait for additional motivation; act within those five seconds.

This rule helps overcome procrastination and creates instant urgency. It bypasses the brain's tendency to overthink and talk you out of taking action. For possum-eating, this could mean using the 5 Second Rule to start a difficult conversation, begin a workout, or take any first step toward your goal.

When our kids were small, we played a game that started each commercial break. When the commercial started, I yelled, "CLEAN UP TIME," and my children sprang into action, cleaning up within the short commercial time, working as quickly as possible. Then, when the commercial break was over, we were back to watching the television show. It was amazing how quickly tasks were accomplished when there was an urgency to do it, and an urgency to complete it so we could watch the television show without any further interruptions. I guarantee you that my children remember those times and will probably pass that urgency of cleaning to their children.

Sometimes, however, urgency can create unwarranted outcomes. We might even overthink the urgency leading to a catastrophic outcome. Remember that obedience and urgency do not have to be catastrophic. It's not time to clean out the pantry and throw away everything. It may be time to talk to someone about why you eat for comfort instead of nourishment. You might want to have your support system help you with a plan to implement and then do it. But first, you must act, and quickly. Since I brought up the whole weight loss thing, it may be nothing but declaring, "I am going to change, and I am going to call my friend who will hold me accountable...and call them right now." Since some people read at 3:00 a.m., there should be some exciting phone calls right now (write to me and tell me about it later—just don't blame me or my publisher!).

#eatthepossum

The point is: DO SOMETHING... AND DO IT IMMEDIATELY. I firmly believe that we are *one yes* away from a better life. One act of obedience will change your destiny. Maybe God is telling you to sell everything and go to Bible College (as I mentioned earlier). That something "RIGHT NOW" may be to talk to someone so they can help you clarify the word of the Lord. I am not discounting that God may tell you to sell everything and move to Congo, but just know that before you go, the first act of obedience will encourage your victory over the next hard thing in your life. In the case of moving to Congo, there is a process you must know before embarking on the journey. That starts with immediate obedience, that with perseverance and faith will give way to victory.

Developing a sense of urgency regarding the hard thing will encourage the additional steps to see them fulfilled. I did it before embarking on my doctoral degree, making the move with urgency. I mentioned my great aunts earlier. My brother had a sense of urgency, which alone inspired the process. Sometimes, once we realize we need to forgive someone, that is when we should forgive them. Thirty-one seconds after we feel the need to forgive may be too late because we begin to justify our actions or inaction. We will relive the moment and reopen the wound. Overthinking is what hinders most acts of immediate obedience.

So, just do it NOW!

Jesus called the disciples to leave everything and follow them. One mentioned that he needed to go to a funeral. Jesus clearly stated that the opportunity for obedience has a particular shelf life. He told him to let the dead bury their dead (Luke 9:60). Why so harsh? Was Jesus uncaring? No, I believe it was because Jesus knew that he would continually procrastinate, argue with his family, try to figure it out, and fight with the devil over the simple command to lay it down and follow Jesus.

We all have that thirty-second window to obey. I wonder how many unforgettable life moments were lost because I failed to act with urgency. Do you wonder the same about your choices? Don't let this one do the same. Do something and do it immediately.

The longer our possum remains, the more our resistance to dealing with it grows. Once, David left his home to fight a foe, but when he returned, his enemies had burned his town of Ziklag to the ground (1 Samuel 30), and David's wives and children were gone. His men's families were also taken captive. Everyone wept until they had no more strength to cry, and then the unthinkable happened: David's men considered stoning David for what had happened to their families. He knew he had to act quickly, so he consulted the ephod, inquired of the Lord, and then received instruction. David wasted no time pursuing those who had caused him so much grief. His obedience and victory were immediate. If David had delayed his obedience, David's enemies might have taken the families to places unknown or, worse, murdered them. For us, urgency is imperative, and immediate obedience is a must. The Lord told David that he would be victorious, and David set out to obey God immediately.

It must be said that David inquired of the Lord, which is imperative to our success. God is for us, not against us. He wants the very best for our lives. I have often said that one of my life's best moments was realizing God has always had my best interest at heart. Every call to obey was for my good, even if it did not seem that way. It is easy to have perfect eyesight when viewing our past, but sometimes when we look back and see the blessing that came to us because of our, "Yes," and our immediate response to God, it will help us in our future endeavors.

There is an excellent example of this in 2 Chronicles 20. Several opposing armies surrounded Jehoshaphat and the people of Judah. They were outnumbered and outgunned (I admit, they did not have guns, only swords and highly skilled warriors). Jehoshaphat immediately sought the Lord and admitted that he did not know what to do. God answered through the prophet and told them they would see God's mighty hand overcome the enemy the next day. Jehoshaphat believed this word from the Lord so much that he gathered the people and assembled one of the largest choirs ever. They went into battle the next day, praising God for victory. Imagine a tiny army walking into a minefield with nothing but worship to God, and you will imagine the actual setting of this story. They're marching and singing delighted God and frustrated the plans of their enemy. They won the victory without one sword, because they inquired of the Lord and immediately obeyed. They obeyed with praise. Such does not make sense, but it is the principle of the kingdom of God: trust, immediately obey, and then watch the enemy fall in defeat. I am sure you are thinking, "Yes, but they waited until the next day. The next day was the day God gave them victory, so they obeyed on the day of God's choosing."

Psalm 119:60 records, "I will hurry, without delay, to obey your commands."

Another example of immediate obedience is in found in Acts 10. Luke records Cornelius' immediate obedience once the angel tells him to find Peter. Immediately, he sends his servants to locate Peter. Because of this, Gentiles have access to the gospel because of a series of moments of immediate obedience, including Peter's immediate obedience. I hate to consider what would have happened if Cornelius or Peter had delayed their obedience. How many will lose eternity because of the delay of obedience in the body of Christ? I shudder to consider the implications.

In Acts 21, the Apostle Paul obeyed God, even though he knew the inevitable outcome would be incarceration and death. He obeyed even when people warned and implored him to forgo his trip to Jerusalem. That obedience put Paul before countless individuals and added credibility to his desire to please God.

It is to be noted that the disciples left their nets and followed Jesus immediately.

Delayed obedience is disobedience.

It also reveals a gap in our trust in God. The longer the wait, the wider the gap of trust.

Our victory is the same. Obey immediately, with urgency, and know that the power of God is greater than your possum.

Imagine what life would have been like if they had immediately obeyed? If you can, you are on your way to the next step in eating the possum: the dream of BBQ possum goodness.

CREATING URGENCY QUESTIONS

1. Reflect on the "thirty-second window of obedience" concept. Can you recall a time when you acted in this window? What was the outcome? Conversely, can you think of a time when you didn't, and what happened?
2. How can you apply the Pomodoro Technique to create urgency in tackling your "possum"? What specific task could you start with using this method?
3. Consider the 5-Second Rule. What immediate action could you take right now towards eating your possum if you applied this rule?
4. Reflect on the story of the Israelites at the edge of the Promised Land. How might their failure to act with urgency relate to challenges you're currently facing?
5. How can you balance the need for urgent action with the wisdom of seeking guidance and planning, as exemplified in the story of Jehoshaphat?

A SUMMARY OF CHAPTER 5 OF *EAT THE POSSUM*:

- **Urgency is Crucial**: Once you've surrounded yourself with the right people, it's time to act quickly on your challenges.
- **The 30-Second Window**: There's a brief window of about thirty seconds to act on God's calling or a decision to change. Procrastination beyond this can lead to failure.
- **Overthinking Leads to Inaction**: The longer you wait, the easier it becomes to talk yourself out of taking action.
- **Techniques for Creating Urgency**:
    1. The Pomodoro Technique: Break work into twenty-minute focused sessions with short breaks.
    2. The 5-Second Rule: Count backward from five to one, then take immediate physical action.
- **Immediate Obedience**: Biblical examples like David, Jehoshaphat, and the disciples demonstrate the power of acting quickly on God's instruction.
- **Delayed Obedience Is Disobedience**: Waiting too long to act can be equivalent to not acting at all.
- **Trust in God**: Immediate obedience reflects trust in God's plan for your life.
- **Balancing Urgency and Wisdom**: While quick action is important, seeking guidance and planning appropriately is crucial, as shown in Jehoshaphat's story.
- **Potential Consequences**: Consider how delayed action might impact you and others around you.
- **Reflection**: The chapter encourages readers to consider their experiences of quick obedience and procrastination and their outcomes.

Remember, the main message is to act quickly and decisively when facing your "possum" (challenge), seek guidance, and maintain faith in the process.

CHAPTER SIX
SAVORING THE POTENTIAL AROMA OF VICTORY

The next step in eating the possum is to envision what life would be like if you actually ate the barbecued possum. On that fateful day, I wasn't sure I had the stomach for such an endeavor. Based on my vivid imagination, I thought I knew what it would taste like, but I had no context, and because of that, I was so wrong. That's the problem with possums. They look like a rat, but they are not in the rat family at all. They are a relative of, wait for it: the kangaroo. It's hard to envision eating a rat, so a little reimagining might be required. If you are to overcome your hard thing, and you can't imagine that you could *ever* overcome it, then you have to dream of what life would be like when you finally overcome it.

I am a dreamer. I dream of vacations, writing books, and cool cars. But I have to see these things to dream of them adequately. I have to envision them by putting them in front of my eyes. I have to see it with my eyes to visualize it in my mind. Others are not so needy when it comes to envisioning things. They can imagine what it would be like without a picture. I can't, so I have coffee mugs, stuffed animals, Christmas ornaments, posters of books, and other items to help me envision what I need to see (most items sold separately at the merch store, www.eatthepos

sum.com). You might be able to envision what life would be like slimmer; I can't imagine it without pictures. For your hard thing to become *no*-thing, you must predict what life would be like if you were to have victory. It may require a poster, a picture, a stuffed animal, or imagining what a restored relationship would be like. It might be a challenge coin with the words "Eat the Possum" embossed on it to solidify your commitment to follow through, or a shirt, refrigerator magnet, or other "eat the possum" worthy item.

I think that is why Jesus told parables in word pictures. He described a Samaritan's situation in word pictures so people could envision what a good neighbor should do. Jesus described a prodigal son's return in word pictures so people could imagine their heavenly Father's response to their return to him (Luke 10:25-37). Over and over again, Jesus painted a picture of an outcome He desired to see in us. We have to do the same! We have to envision what life would be like if we saw victory.

So, how do you paint the picture of what life would be like to see a victory? I couldn't view my barbecue as a rodent, and I had to understand that I would not die if I ate the possum. Most everyone at the wild game barbecue tasted everything, including the possum, without catastrophic sickness sweeping through the banquet hall. There was not a mad dash to the restrooms or garbage cans. I had to envision eating the possum and enjoying every bite, smiling without gagging, and putting every taunter back in their place. To do that, I had to change my mindset. How is this accomplished? Sometimes, it is done in our minds.

The Apostle Paul said that we should not conform to this world but be transformed by changing "the way you think" (Romans 12:1-2). Interestingly, Paul did not encourage us to change *what* we were thinking, but *the "way"* we were thinking. Why is this important? If we change *what* we are thinking, we are merely diverting our minds to something else. The old pathways to the problem remain. We may start off well, but our well-worn pathways will take us back to the same place. However, the pathways that brought us to *that* thought process and the eventual outcome of that process must change if we are to overcome our hard things. Think of it this way: Imagine a massive forest in front of you, and to your right is a sign that says, "Steak and Potato Trail." I personally love this trail. It is a well-worn path, because it is *the way* you get from one side of the forest to the opposite side with delicious abandon. Since you have always traveled that path, you can navigate its trails with your eyes closed.

But also imagine an adventure available for anyone who was willing to forgo the well-worn path for a new one. It would be challenging, because there are thistles and briars, low-hanging branches, creeks, rivers, hills, valleys, and scrub brush along the way, and you will have to be mindful of where you are going and the path you took to get there, or else you might get lost. You may even dread the prospect of such an endeavor and refuse to start. That's why it is important to see the outcome before the adventure begins.

But what if, nestled within the folds of your imagination, lay a path less traveled, one that unfurls amidst the most breathtaking vistas imaginable? Envision a journey that winds through verdant valleys, where the air is crisp and the silence speaks volumes, bordered by majestic mountains crowned with pristine, snow-capped peaks. Along this path, imagine encountering enchanting waterfalls, their crystal waters cascading from dizzying heights, feeding into a serene stream that meanders gently below. This stream, a lifeline to the lush flora that flanks its banks, nurtures an explosion of greenery and vibrant wildflowers, painting a scene so vivid it almost seems surreal.

This is a view your well-trodden path could never reveal, hidden as it was by the cloak of familiarity and the dullness of routine. But by daring to venture onto this new trail, you've not only discovered a world of untold beauty but also a strength within yourself you might not have known existed. Having conquered the challenges of this off-beaten path, the idea of embarking on another wilderness adventure next time you seek to traverse the forest seems not just appealing, but exhilarating.

Indeed, the thrill of overcoming these obstacles, of witnessing nature's unspoiled splendor, may stir a profound desire within you—a yearning to chase these experiences for a lifetime. It's not just a journey; it's a transformation, one that reshapes your understanding of what it means to truly live and explore. This path, once new and daunting, now stands as a testament to the joy of discovery and the boundless possibilities that lie in choosing the road less traveled.

It might just become addictive to attempt great things.

You have just envisioned eating a possum.

Now, take what you are dreading and envision new paths, vistas, and opportunities. Make a picture or a poster, get a stuffed animal (but no voodoo dolls, please), and use those items to help you dream of what life would be like when you eat the possum, because I can assure you that it is not nearly as bad as you think and might just change the way you think about hard things.

Think for a minute about Moses and the burning bush in the Old Testament. God was about to call a man who had been shepherding sheep for over forty years to go back to the place where he had killed an Egyptian because of his treatment of the Jews.

If Moses were to read the job description for what God was going to call him to accomplish, it might just read something like this:

JOB DESCRIPTION: LEADER OF THE EXODUS

Location: Egypt
Destination: Canaan (Promised Land)
About Us:

We are an emerging nation currently based in Egypt, on the cusp of realizing our destiny of liberation and returning to the homeland promised to our ancestors. Our community is built upon the pillars of slavery, tradition, and a profound commitment to vocalizing our grievances. We are on the lookout for a steadfast and committed individual to steer us from our captivity in Egypt to the freedom awaiting us in our ancestral land.

Job Summary:

The Leader of the Exodus will play a pivotal role in guiding, managing, and protecting our people through a daunting expedition from Egypt to Canaan. This position demands a solid connection with God, unwavering faith, and superior leadership abilities. The ideal candidate will exhibit exceptional communication skills, a distinguished history of leading through trials, and the capability to perform miracles as needed.

Key Responsibilities:

- Negotiate the liberation of our people with the Egyptian Pharaoh.
- Navigate the nation through the wilderness, including the passage through the Red Sea.
- Act as the chief liaison between God and the people, facilitating the delivery of laws and commandments.
- Ensure the provision of food and water for the nation, including the sourcing of miraculous sustenance as necessary.
- Implement and uphold divine laws and standards within the community, as communicated directly by God.
- Address and ameliorate conflicts within the community, fostering a united and faithful congregation despite prevalent discontent.

- Supervise the construction and upkeep of the Ark of the Covenant and the Tabernacle, serving as symbols of the God's presence amongst us.
- Cultivate and ready the next cadre of leaders for their eventual conquest of the Promised Land.

Qualifications:

- Demonstrated proficiency in leadership, negotiation, and conflict resolution.
- Strong communication skills with a knack for persuasive discourse to both individuals and large assemblies.
- A verified history of miracle-working or an earnest readiness to adopt such skills.
- A deep and personal connection with God, inclusive of receiving direct revelations and instructions.
- Resilience, patience, and stamina to lead a prolonged and arduous journey across varied landscapes.
- Irrefutable integrity and a dedicated allegiance to the divine mandate.

This position is not just a job; it's a calling. If you have the faith, leadership skills, and the determination to lead a nation to its divine destiny, we want to hear from you.

Can you imagine seeing such a posting? Answering the call for this job posting would have left Moses shaking his head. For Moses, his qualifications were pretty much, "I lead sheep, I once murdered a guy, and I have a little bit of training in Pharoah's house."

One can imagine that Moses felt woefully unqualified. It was too hard. But when God called Moses, he painted a picture of the outcome.

Here is the story:

One day, Moses was tending the flock of his father-in-law,

Jethro, the priest of Midian. He led the flock farther into the wilderness and came to Sinai, the mountain of God. There, the angel of the LORD appeared to him in a blazing fire from the middle of a bush. Moses stared in amazement. Though the bush was engulfed in flames, it didn't burn up. "This is amazing," Moses said to himself. "Why isn't that bush burning up? I must go see it."

When the LORD saw Moses coming to take a closer look, God called to him from the middle of the bush, "Moses! Moses!"

"Here I am!" Moses replied.

"Do not come any closer," the LORD warned. "Take off your sandals, for you are standing on holy ground. I am the God of your father[1]*—the God of Abraham, the God of Isaac, and the God of Jacob." When Moses heard this, he covered his face because he was afraid to look at God.

Then the LORD told him, "I have certainly seen the oppression of my people in Egypt. I have heard their cries of distress because of their harsh slave drivers. Yes, I am aware of their suffering. *So, I have come down to rescue them from the power of the Egyptians and lead them out of Egypt into their own fertile and spacious land. It is a land flowing with milk and honey—the land where the Canaanites, Hittites, Amorites, Perizzites, Hivites, and Jebusites now live (emphasis mine).* Look! The cry of the people of Israel has reached me, and I have seen how harshly the Egyptians abuse them. Now go, for I am sending you to Pharaoh. You must lead my people, Israel, out of Egypt." (Exodus 3:1-10)

So now you see a word picture God painted for Moses before the big reveal, similar to sitting in front of a plate of uncertain barbecue meat, wondering what it all meant. Let's go a little further:

"Now go and call together all the elders of Israel. Tell them, 'Yahweh, the God of your ancestors—the God of Abraham, Isaac, and Jacob—has appeared to me. He told me, 'I have been

---

1. * **3:6** Greek version reads *your fathers.*

watching closely, and I see how the Egyptians are treating you. I have promised to rescue you from your oppression in Egypt. *I will lead you to a land flowing with milk and honey—the land where the Canaanites, Hittites, Amorites, Perizzites, Hivites, and Jebusites now live.'"*

So, let's get this straight: Moses is hiding on the back side of the desert, herding sheep for forty years because he murdered a guy. God calls him to go back to the place of the murder, not to confess, but to confront. He is going to face the king, the supreme ruler, the one the Egyptian people believe to be a god, and he will tell Pharoah that the *real* God has sent to tell him that Pharoah *will* let the people of God go free. Moses will challenge him, and God will show up every time in increasingly bad situations.

Until the last and worst one, Moses must follow specific directions, or people will die. Moses will have to let the Jews know what they are supposed to do and tell them that he will lead them to the land that God promised the patriarch Abraham. It will be through a desert where there is no drinking water, barren land where there is no food to kill and eat, and it will stretch any leadership skills Moses might have.

We know of nothing in his life that qualified him to lead more than a few sheep, certainly not the few hundred thousand two-year-olds he ended up leading. I have raised three two-year-olds; it was the most challenging twelve years of my life.

Hard things rarely come to qualified people; otherwise, they would not be difficult. The key was to keep the vision in front of Moses; the same is true for you.

Imagine life after overcoming your hard thing. For example, if your possum is your weight, imagine what life would be like if you were healthier. Write it down. List the benefits. Envision the outcome. Make a poster.

It will be hard and may require a miracle, but God can give you victory. See it, pray for it, and write it down.

It *is* too hard, and the God of all creation knows it better than you; that's why He called you to do it. I have heard all the excuses, too. When asking someone to serve in an area where there is inadequate help, they will say, "I don't know how," or "It's too hard," or "I have never been trained." Those statements sound pious, almost honorable, and self-effacing. But they are unbiblical.

Where did God call the qualified? Was it Peter, a foolish, impetuous fisherman? Later, the "experts" asked of Peter and his equally unqualified colleagues, "Who are these foolish and unlearned men? They are turning the world upside down" (Acts 4:13).

Was it David when God had the prophet anoint him as a young teenager? He didn't even look the part, and no one else "saw it in him." But God did!

Or what about Jesus? God did not send Him to be born in the castle, but in a cave. He didn't surround him with the elite and pomp at His birth (although the angels and shepherds were pretty awesome). He didn't even put him in a home that was altogether perfect, because Mary had to tell her soon-to-be husband that she was pregnant by the power of God. Think about how hard that was! But in each of these, they envisioned something better. For Moses, God painted the picture. Peter saw the resurrected savior, and he was never the same. David became a man after God's heart and envisioned a more incredible shepherd who watched over his life. And Jesus obeyed the Father, doing the most challenging thing ever in the history of humanity, when he, "for the joy that was set before Him, endured the cross and despised its shame," (Hebrews 12:2) doing the hardest thing known to mankind to win our salvation.

Try this vision exercise to begin the process of seeing things differently. I will call it Possum Vision.

Practice this visualization regularly, especially when you feel discouraged. Let the image of transforming your "possum" into something positive reinforce your belief in your ability to overcome challenges.

BIBLICAL POSSUM VISION: SEEING GOD'S VICTORY

Find a quiet place where you won't be disturbed. Begin with prayer, asking God for guidance and wisdom. Then meditate on these steps:

1. Acknowledge Your Current Situation:
    - Visualize your 'possum'—the challenge you're facing. Reflect on Psalm 139:23-24: "Search me, God, and know my heart; test me and know my anxious thoughts."
2. Envision God's Transformation:
    - Picture your challenge being transformed by God's power. Remember Isaiah 43:19: "See, I am doing a new thing! Now it springs up; do you not perceive it? I am making a way in the wilderness and streams in the wasteland."
3. See Your Victory in Christ:
    - Imagine yourself approaching this transformed challenge with confidence in Christ. Meditate on Philippians 4:13: "I can do all things through Christ who strengthens me."
4. Reflect on God's Faithfulness:
    - Envision the aftermath of overcoming this challenge. Consider Joshua 1:9: "Have I not commanded you? Be strong and courageous. Do not be afraid; do not be discouraged, for the Lord your God will be with you wherever you go."
5. Embrace Your Future in God's Plan:
    - Picture your future self, having overcome this challenge. Reflect on Jeremiah 29:11: "'For I know the plans I have for you,' declares the Lord, 'plans to prosper you and not to harm you, plans to give you hope and a future.'"

6. Return with Renewed Faith:
    - Slowly open your eyes, carrying the peace and confidence of God's promises with you.
    Remember Romans 8:28: "And we know that in all things God works for the good of those who love him, who have been called according to his purpose."

In each of these, God provided a picture of what life would be like once the hard thing was accomplished. That's what you should do next:

Dream big because God does that just for you!

This is the best place to begin to formulate a plan for eating your possum.

Note the personality types and the best way each should approach their challenge:

ANALYTICAL ALEX (THINKER)

Alex should approach challenging problems by:

- Creating a detailed decision matrix to evaluate potential solutions.
- Setting strict deadlines for each phase of problem-solving to avoid analysis paralysis.
- Collaborating with others to gain diverse perspectives and challenge his own assumptions.

Strategy: Alex could emulate Paul's approach by writing structured arguments for and against each potential solution, helping him reach a logical conclusion.

PRINCIPLED PAULA (PERSISTER)

Paula can overcome challenges by:

- Aligning problem-solving strategies with her core values.
- Creating a personal mission statement that incorporates growth and adaptability.
- Seeking guidance from respected mentors who share her principles.

Approach: Like Daniel, Paula should stand firm in her convictions while remaining open to new ideas that align with her values.

EMPATHETIC EMMA (HARMONIZER)

Emma might tackle difficult problems by:

- Reframing challenges as opportunities to better support her community.
- Forming a support group to share experiences and solutions.
- Balancing her empathy for others with self-care practices.

Tactic: Emma could follow Mary's example by considering how overcoming her challenges could positively impact those around her.

CHARISMATIC CHARLIE (PROMOTER)

Charlie should plan for success by:

- Breaking down large problems into exciting, short-term challenges.
- Creating a public commitment to solving the problem, leveraging his charisma to gather support.
- Celebrating small victories to maintain momentum.

Method: Like Peter, Charlie should use his enthusiasm to rally others around his cause, creating a supportive network for problem-solving.

SPONTANEOUS SAM (REBEL)

Sam can approach challenges by:

- Developing unconventional solutions that challenge traditional problem-solving methods.
- Setting up a reward system that appeals to his desire for novelty and excitement.
- Reframing problem-solving as an act of rebellion against limitations.

Strategy: Sam should channel Samson's rebellious energy into creative problem-solving, turning challenges into opportunities for innovation.

CONTEMPLATIVE CORY (IMAGINER)

Cory might overcome problems by:

- Visualizing the desired outcome in detail to maintain motivation.
- Breaking down abstract ideas into concrete, actionable steps.
- Using journaling or art to explore different aspects of the problem.

Approach: Like John, Cory should use his rich inner world to gain deep insights into the problem, then translate these visions into practical solutions.

AMBITIOUS AVA (ACHIEVER)

Ava can plan for success by:

- Setting clear, measurable goals with specific timelines.
- Creating a detailed action plan with milestones to track progress.
- Balancing her drive for achievement with self-care practices to prevent burnout.

Tactic: Following Nehemiah's example, Ava should approach problem-solving with determination and strategic planning.

INTUITIVE IAN (DISCERNER)

Ian should tackle challenges by:

- Trusting his intuition to identify the root causes of problems.
- Developing a flexible problem-solving framework that allows for intuitive insights.
- Practicing mindfulness to enhance his intuitive abilities.

Method: Like Jeremiah, Ian should balance his deep insights with practical action, trusting his intuition while taking concrete steps.

ADVENTUROUS ANDY (EXPLORER)

Andy can overcome problems by:

- Approaching challenges as exciting new territories to explore.
- Seeking out diverse experiences that might offer novel solutions.
- Creating a flexible problem-solving plan that allows for spontaneity.

Strategy: Following Abraham's example, Andy should embrace the unknown aspects of his challenges, viewing them as opportunities for growth and discovery.

CAUTIOUS CATHY (QUESTIONER)

Cathy might plan for success by:

- Conducting thorough research on potential solutions and their outcomes.
- Creating a detailed risk assessment for each approach.
- Developing a series of small experiments to test solutions before full implementation.

Approach: Like Thomas, Cathy should use her skepticism as a tool for rigorous problem-solving, seeking evidence-based solutions.

DIPLOMATIC DAN (PEACEMAKER)

Dan can tackle challenges by:

- Identifying all stakeholders affected by the problem and considering their perspectives.
- Developing collaborative solutions that address multiple concerns.
- Creating a communication plan to ensure all parties feel heard and valued.

Tactic: Following Barnabas's example, Dan should use his mediation skills to find solutions that create harmony and mutual benefit.

ORGANIZED OLIVIA (GUARDIAN)

Olivia should approach problems by:

- Creating a detailed, step-by-step action plan with clear deadlines.
- Developing contingency plans for potential obstacles.
- Establishing a structured review process to track progress and make adjustments.

Method: Like Esther, Olivia should leverage her organizational skills to create and execute a well-structured problem-solving strategy.

VISIONARY VICTOR (INNOVATIVE THINKER)

Victor can plan for success by:

- Brainstorming multiple innovative approaches to the problem.
- Creating a holistic strategy that addresses interconnected issues.
- Developing a flexible framework that allows for pivoting as new information emerges.

Strategy: Following Moses's example, Victor should maintain a grand vision while breaking it down into manageable, interconnected steps.

SUPPORTIVE SARAH (COUNSELOR)

Sarah might overcome challenges by:

- Developing a self-care routine to maintain her emotional resilience.
- Creating a personal growth plan that aligns with her values of supporting others.
- Forming a mutual support network to exchange ideas and encouragement.

Approach: Like Priscilla, Sarah should balance her supportive nature with self-development, recognizing that personal growth enhances her ability to help others.

For all of these personality types, use some type of visual for success.

A SUMMARY OF CHAPTER 6 FOR *EAT THE POSSUM*:

- **Envisioning Success**: The chapter emphasizes the importance of visualizing success to overcome difficult challenges, using the metaphor of eating barbecued possum. It suggests that envisioning the outcome can help in tackling seemingly impossible tasks.
- **Imagination and Visualization**: The author discusses different ways people visualize their goals. Some need physical items like pictures or objects to help them imagine success, while others can visualize outcomes without such aids.
- **Biblical Parables as Examples**: The chapter references how Jesus used parables to help people envision moral lessons, suggesting that creating

mental images can guide individuals toward achieving their goals.
- **Changing Mindsets**: The text highlights the need to change not just what we think, but *how* we think. This involves creating new mental pathways rather than relying on old ones.
- **Overcoming Challenges**: The chapter uses a metaphorical journey through a forest to illustrate the concept of taking a less-traveled path, which, although challenging, can lead to greater rewards and personal growth.
- **Biblical References**: The story of Moses and the burning bush is used to illustrate how God provided a vision for overcoming daunting tasks, reinforcing the idea that envisioning success is crucial.
- **Practical Visualization Exercise**: A step-by-step guide called "Possum Vision" is provided to help readers visualize overcoming their challenges by seeing God's victory in their lives.
- **Personality Types and Approaches**: The chapter outlines different personality types and suggests tailored strategies for each type to approach challenges effectively. These include methods for thinkers, harmonizers, promoters, rebels, and more.
- **Encouragement to Dream Big**: The chapter concludes by encouraging readers to dream big and use visualization as a tool to formulate plans for tackling their own "possums," or difficult challenges.

CHAPTER SEVEN

POSSUM PICNIC: SPREADING THE FEAST AND TAKING NAMES

I have something to share with you that might just freak you completely out: There are likely possums within one hundred yards of you right now. They are hiding in your backyard, out of sight, until their moment of dumpster diving arrives. This brings us to an important aspect of your hard thing: it may harbor secrets.

There is an unknown aspect of your possum that will show up at just the right time to derail your attempt to overcome your hard thing. More times than I can count, when I have attempted a great thing, suddenly something happens that attempts to derail me, discourage me, overwhelm me to give up trying.

WHEN FAITH MEETS THE POSSUM: A PASTOR'S TALE

In 2013, I faced my own giant possum. Our church had been hit with a double whammy: we lost a property we were trying to purchase due to an unexpected lien, and, on the same day, we lost the lease on our current building. In one fell swoop, we went from having a stable church home to becoming nomads.

Over the next year, we bounced between four different locations in just seven weeks. The possum of discouragement was staring me down, and I was ready to play dead. Friends "encouraged" me to quit, insisting no one would follow us through this chaos. I believed them.

One dismal, cold, rainy Sunday, I was ready to throw in the towel. We were meeting in an elementary school cafeteria, and fifteen minutes before the service, only the set-up crew was present. I confessed my despair to them, admitting I felt no one would show up. But I made a decision: "Regardless of who comes, we will worship, and I will preach like the house is full."

We started the service with a mere fifteen people. I pushed through my doubts. I opened in prayer and began greeting attendees. Suddenly, one of our crew members interrupted me, urgently requesting more chairs. I was confused; we had set up forty chairs, far more than I expected.

Then I saw it: over one hundred people were streaming into the cafeteria. We broke our attendance record for the entire year, surpassing even Easter and Mother's Day.

In that moment, I realized I had been ready to succumb to the possum of despair. Instead, by choosing to push forward despite my fears, I witnessed a miracle. I had to excuse myself to repent for my lack of faith. On that day, I ate more crow than possum, but facing the hard thing taught me that the biggest possums often come right before our greatest breakthroughs. When you're faced with your possum moment:

1. Acknowledge your fears, but don't let them paralyze you.
2. Commit to moving forward, even if you can't see the outcome.
3. Surround yourself with supportive people who will pray for and encourage you.
4. Be prepared for unexpected blessings when you choose to "eat the possum."
5. Anticipate a setback regardless!

The secret we discovered was that if God is in it, even setbacks are opportunities for God to move in our lives. Setbacks are steppingstones for people of faith, but beware: in every advancement and in most setbacks, imposing secrets threaten to derail us.

The one seeking weight loss may learn they are diabetic, and suddenly their attempt to lose weight has the added pressure of the health issue. The one wanting to give more to the church learn their job is being phased out. Every attempt of advancement holds some type of secret that threatens the vision God has given.

Colonel Sanders of KFC fame is a case study in overcoming setbacks. Harland Sanders (Colonel) was born in 1890 and faced numerous setbacks throughout his life. He worked various jobs, including as a streetcar conductor, insurance salesman, and service station operator. His secret possum revealed itself to Sanders at the age of sixty-five. He had opened a restaurant, and the new Interstate 75 bypassed his restaurant, causing his business to fail. This could have been the end of his career, but it revealed a hidden opportunity.

OVERCOMING HARDNESS AVERSION:

Instead of giving up, Sanders decided to franchise his chicken recipe. He traveled across the U.S., cooking chicken for restaurant owners. He was rejected 1,009 times before his first success.

DISCOVERING HIDDEN STRENGTHS:

Through this process, Sanders discovered his true strengths:

- Resilience in the face of rejection
- Belief in his product
- Ability to adapt his business model

His breakthrough moment came in 1964, at the age of seventy-four, when he sold Kentucky Fried Chicken Corporation for $2 million (equivalent to about $17 million today). The company he started became a global fast-food chain.

The lessons Colonel Sanders learned included age is not a barrier to success; setbacks can reveal hidden opportunities. Persistence is the key to overcoming challenges; and adapting your approach can lead to unexpected success.

Ask virtually any Old Testament or New Testament character who desired to do something for God, and you will find a similar story. When you lead a million people in the desert, and you will probably run out of water with no prospects for hydration within miles, the secret to an amazing victory is within striking distance. These "hidden possums" were not problems as much as they were opportunities for God to do something amazing.

Secrets are everywhere, much like the possum. Some are secret answers, but others are insidious. They crop up like dandelions in a beautiful yard, spreading their root system everywhere. Some reveal our true friends and expose our enemies. They reveal themselves with impeccable timing. Just know that when you begin the process of overcoming your hard thing, you will encounter a battle that can stop you in your tracks.

What are some secrets that may derail your hard thing?

First, underlying fears are insidious secrets that are revealed when we start the process of change. Fear of failure, change, or success can sabotage progress. Recognizing and addressing these fears is crucial to success.

Second, perfectionism can hinder progress. For example, we might want to wait for the right moment or seek to achieve a goal with no room for error, which can lead to paralysis by analysis. Perfectionism often results in inaction. Perfectionism also creates an unreasonable and unhealthy expectation that will always derail you. Some quit before beginning because it is impossible to achieve the resulting goal. I love writing and know that I will probably write multiple books before I find traction with one and sell enough to do more than buy a latte at a high-priced coffee house. If perfectionism creates an unreasonable standard, I will quit before I begin. That perfectionism keeps a lot of brilliant people from overcoming the hardest things in life.

Third, a failure to adapt to unforeseen circumstances can hinder the progress of the very strategic among us. Learning to pivot when necessary can provide a path to success that the original path never offered.

Next, an overemphasis on the outcome can rob us of an important experience on the journey. When I embarked on my doctoral journey, I desired to learn as much as I could about the subject of strategic change. Honestly, I looked forward to the day when they called me "Dr. John Utley.: What I discovered, however, was that I learned more about myself than I did about the subject. I thoroughly enjoyed the journey, because it became a journey of learning why I do the things I do, some good and some bad. That was worth the price of admission. If you are so focused on the destination, you miss the journey, and the most important lessons you can learn are those. I say this even to those who struggle with diet issues. Some fight their way to a goal and miss the beauty of the journey of healthy living.

Sometimes it is the journey that matters most.

So far, we have highlighted other areas that may harbor secret places that sidetrack us, such as procrastination, lack of vision, isolation, accountability, etc. There are secrets, however, that may reveal pitfalls and enemies that you never knew existed before you started. These are instructive and should not be underestimated. Some secrets may not be revealed to you before they are revealed to others. Mostly, these are benign, but sometimes they may be used against you. They are blind spots that others may see before you.

But here is an important warning: Not everyone has your best interest at heart, and your secret, once revealed, may be fodder for their war against you.

Those are strong terms to use, but not everyone handles secrets well. When people around you are true friends, they help you see the blind spots, and once you reveal those blind spots, they can help you overcome your hard things. Others are not so kind or helpful. In fact, they may leverage your secret into shame.

Here is a real-life example:

Years ago, I worked at a hospital. One day, one of the supervisors in our department went to the restroom, roughly one hundred feet away from the kitchen. We know that because of what happened afterward. When she returned, she harbored a secret she wasn't even privy to, because the strongest toilet paper known to humanity was somehow caught in her clothing. She had toilet paper waist high, trailing her down a hallway still connected to the end of the roll. Every step she took was an advertisement for her previous location and the strength of the toilet paper. She was oblivious to the problem behind her that was about to set her up for embarrassment. Unfortunately, no one chased her down and helped her forgo the consequences of her secret. She needed a friend who could discreetly point out her blind spot and help her without a problem. But no one came to her aid.

So get this picture: a supervisor who was always hard on those she supervised returned to the kitchen with toilet paper waist high, one hundred feet long, still attached to the roll in the restroom.

One of the crudest workers on the tray line caught a glimpse of her secret and called out, "Hey, where have you been?"

"None of your business. Get back to work," she snapped.

Then he started singing, "I know where you have been... we all know... it's the place... where you go...." He laughed so hard that everyone stopped what they were doing and looked at him and then at the supervisor. He sang the same lyrics again in a sing-song fashion, but she was still oblivious to why he was making fun of her. Finally, someone said, "Look behind you," and with that, she whirled around to find her faithful follower: the most robust toilet paper in the world. She was so embarrassed, and everyone chided the worker for his cruelty.

The important point is that your secret may need revelation, but your success will depend on whether a trusted friend reveals it, one who will not leverage your secret against you, or one who will exploit it against you.

I can testify that she wished she had a friend who would have told her, "You are being followed! You can't see the danger in your past! You have a secret that will hurt you."

She was blind to her own issue, but someone who was *not* her friend leveraged her problem for their own benefit.

I haven't thought of that story until now. I believe the Holy Spirit wants you to know that you are being followed by something in your life that will cause you pain, humiliation, drama, and hurt. It may not reveal itself until you begin the process of overcoming your possum. Sometimes, people want to exploit it, make sport of your blind spot, and use it against you. Worse yet, this nagging voice in the back of your head cries out that the thing that follows you also disqualifies you. It is the thing that will forever keep you from doing anything for God. That voice uses the taunt to drive the shame deep into your heart until you give up before you start, debilitated even before you know it. Jesus wants to reveal it to you so you can know what is going on and get healed, which will look surprisingly like you are free from the issue.

Another example comes from one of the Bible's most famous confrontations. Those who found the woman in the act of adultery were not concerned about her secret; they wanted to leverage it against her and Jesus (John 8:1-11). Jesus didn't fall for it, and neither should you. Many around you want to leverage your secret against you, and if Satan is involved in that secret at all, he will do his best to leverage it against the work of God.

Jesus had a secret, too. His secret, evidently known by Satan, was that He was the Messiah. This is not a bad secret, but one that was to be revealed at the most opportune time. He also did not want the father of lies to be the one testifying to this truth. At His temptation, Satan attempted to leverage that secret against Jesus so that Jesus disobeyed the will of the Father. Disobedience to the Father would have destroyed mankind's only hope of salvation.

Jesus overcame the enemy by remembering and reciting the words of His Father. We must do the same, but not necessarily the words from our earthly father. For most, the words of our earthly fathers are not helpful. Many have shared the hurtful words of their earthly fathers. Once, a friend told me his father called him "stupid" at a young age. My friend never forgot those words, and they have informed virtually everything he has attempted since. In his case, I shared that the words of his Heavenly Father were more beneficial to his development than his earthly father. My father never told me I was stupid, but I can remember when my earthly father told me he was proud of me, at least the first time I recall. I was forty-two years old when he told me this vital thing. It was about four months before my father died.

While it is a decisive moment when our earthly father says he is proud or calls out something good in our life, Satan will seek to frustrate how we perceive the way God sees us. Satan will do everything he can to leverage the words of those around us to inform the way we view God or the way we perceive that He views us. That is not to say God affirms every action in our lives, because God does not. His standards are standards of holiness, and He does not deviate from His standards. He calls us to those standards with the empowerment and love to help us reach His standards. Sometimes we need to hear affirmations from God, and sometimes we need to be corrected. Both are powerful and mitigate the attempts of the enemy to leverage our faults against us. This is probably the best place to state the incredible truth that Scripture notes: "a loving father corrects his children" (Hebrews 12:6). God's children should surrender to the will of God and obey Him completely. Otherwise, the enemy of our soul will exploit our lack of obedience in such a way that will be catastrophic in this life and damnable in the next.

As I noted earlier, people sometimes leverage your secrets against you. Sometimes, you will also see the weaknesses and faults of others. In our selfish state, we can manipulate them to our advantage. We can exploit them to humiliate others. We may even see a legitimate need to call attention to the fault, but doing so incorrectly may be spiritually catastrophic for their growth, and ours.

The Apostle Paul wrote:

> Brothers, if anyone is caught in any transgression, you who are spiritual should restore him in a spirit of gentleness. Keep watch on yourself, lest you too be tempted. Bear one another's burdens, and so fulfill the law of Christ. For if anyone thinks he is something, when he is nothing, he deceives himself. (Galatians 6:1-3, ESV)

If you see a fault in others, restore them. I believe the same thing goes for anything we can exploit in others to bring them shame.

While walking with toilet paper stuck in your pants is not a transgression, it can bring humiliation when exposed. Sometimes, just being a good person and helping people navigate through life without too much difficulty will help you experience an abundant life. You see, the possums in your life thrive on anonymity, just as secrets are emboldened through a similar anonymity.

This shows itself powerfully as we reveal the possum in our lives, which leads us to a most vulnerable place.

How does one find the hidden possums?

In chapter 1, we identified the "you" factor as the best place to look. These hidden possums are potential weaknesses based on your personality type. Once you identify your personality type, you can access your key characteristics and potential weaknesses in facing challenges. Consider these as possible hidden possums in your life. Finally, note the strategies for improvement of your particular type.

Here are some hidden challenges these personality types might encounter:

Analytical Alex, the Thinker, might struggle with emotional situations that require intuition rather than logic, often overlooking practical details while focusing on abstract concepts.

Principled Paula, the Persister, may find it difficult to adapt to necessary changes and risks, becoming judgmental towards those with different values.

Empathetic Emma, the Harmonizer, could be vulnerable to emotional manipulation and struggle with setting personal boundaries.

Charismatic Charlie, the Promoter, tends to overlook important details in pursuit of excitement and may have difficulty maintaining long-term relationships.

Spontaneous Sam, the Rebel, often struggles with authority figures and structured environments, potentially alienating others due to unpredictable behavior.

Contemplative Cory, the Imaginer, might become isolated from others due to their rich inner world and struggle with practical, day-to-day tasks.

Ambitious Ava, the Achiever, risks defining self-worth solely through achievements, potentially compromising ethics in pursuit of success.

Intuitive Ian (Discerner) may struggle to explain complex inner thoughts and withdraw from social situations due to overstimulation.

Adventurous Andy, the Explorer, might find it hard to commit to one path or career, missing out on depth of experience due to the constant pursuit of novelty.

Cautious Cathy, the Questioner, could suffer from paralysis by analysis, leading to missed opportunities and difficulty trusting others.

Diplomatic Dan, the Peacemaker, tends to suppress his own needs to maintain harmony, risking resentment due to constant compromise.

Organized Olivia, the Guardian, might struggle with unexpected changes and become inflexible or resistant to innovation.

Visionary Victor (Innovative Thinker) often starts many projects but finishes few, struggling with routine tasks while overlooking important details.

Lastly, **Supportive Sarah, the Counselor,** tends to take on others' problems as her own, potentially neglecting personal needs due to focus on others.

Recognizing these hidden challenges is the next step in eating the possum. By acknowledging and addressing these potential pitfalls, each personality type can turn their unique traits into powerful tools for personal growth and success.

Once you envision what eating the possum will be like, you must do the next step. In my opinion, this could be the hardest. You have to tell somebody what you are about to do.

CHAPTER 7 QUESTIONS:

1. What "secret possums" or hidden challenges have you encountered in your past attempts at personal growth or change? How did they impact your progress?
2. How can you apply the lessons from the pastor's church relocation story to your own situation when facing unexpected setbacks?
3. Reflecting on Colonel Sanders' story, how might your current challenges or setbacks be hiding potential opportunities for growth or success?
4. Among the "insidious secrets" mentioned (underlying fears, perfectionism, failure to adapt, overemphasis on outcomes), which do you think poses the greatest threat to your personal change journey? Why?
5. How can you distinguish between supportive friends who help you see your blind spots and those who might exploit your vulnerabilities? What steps can you take to surround yourself with the former?
6. Considering the "you" factor and the personality types discussed, what potential hidden challenges or weaknesses might you encounter during your change journey? How can you proactively tackle these?
7. The chapter emphasizes the importance of revealing your intentions to someone. Who in your life could you trust to share your goals with, and how might this accountability help you in overcoming your "possum"?

A SUMMARY OF CHAPTER 7 OF *EAT THE POSSUM*:

- Hidden challenges, or "secret possums," often emerge when attempting to overcome difficult obstacles.
- These unexpected setbacks can derail progress if not properly addressed.

- The chapter uses a pastor's experience with church relocation as an example of overcoming discouragement and unexpected challenges.
- Colonel Sanders' story is presented as a case study in persistence and adapting to setbacks.
- Several types of "insidious secrets" that can hinder progress are identified:
  1. Underlying fears.
  2. Perfectionism.
  3. Failure to adapt.
  4. Overemphasis on outcomes.
- The importance of the journey, not just the destination, is emphasized in personal growth.
- Not everyone has your best interests at heart; some may use your vulnerabilities against you.
- The chapter stresses the importance of having supportive friends who can help identify blind spots without exploiting them.
- Different personality types may face unique hidden challenges in their personal growth journeys.
- Recognizing and addressing these potential pitfalls can turn unique traits into tools for success.
- The chapter concludes by emphasizing the importance of sharing your intentions with someone trustworthy as a crucial step in overcoming your "possum."
- Readers are encouraged to reflect on their own experiences with hidden challenges and how they can apply the lessons from the chapter to their personal growth journeys.

CHAPTER EIGHT

POSSUM POTLUCK: SHARING YOUR CATCH

A t this point of eating the possum, you need to tell a trusted friend that you are going to eat the possum. For example, if your goal is to finish high school, college, or the thing you always wanted to complete but didn't because it was too hard, you must tell someone what you will try to do. This is the hardest, because your secret desire is about to become known.

Earlier, we mentioned the individuals you need to surround yourself with, and they play a massive part in this step. The one that sees you for who you can be, not just who you have been. The one who can speak the truth in love. The one who has your back, a friend who has your best interests in mind. You *must* tell them what your possum is and that you need their support, accountability, and encouragement to see victory. This is where the type of person you surround yourself with meets the specific reason they are around you: to help you eat your possum.

For example, if you want to lose weight, you will be more likely to see victory if you surround yourself with support, accountability, and encouragement. They must know your goal to fulfill their support role successfully.

Why do you tell them at this stage, and not earlier? It takes time to determine who will be your allies, and telling people prematurely may hinder your success. You have to be prepared for the moment you tell them. Initially, they may question your decision and may even oppose it. If you are not ready to embark on this journey with determination, you can't expect people around you to mirror your optimism.

So, with whom do you share your possum challenge?

Do not look for people who are unsupportive of your goal, as they can sabotage your progress. I once experienced the power of an unsupportive partner when a couple was not successful in supporting one another. The wife wanted to quit smoking. She felt it was necessary, but her husband continued to obstruct her attempts to overcome the addiction. He was not supportive at all. Others have shared stories of trying to lose weight only to have a "supporting" family member show up with donuts for breakfast.

You should know that accountability is not a police matter either. A loving accountability partner will ask you questions about your progress, help you see the obstacles in your pursuit of success, and cheer you on. They are not to police your actions or your life. They are to help you stay strong and to help you know that you have someone in your corner looking out for your best interests. They will be loving, remind you of your possum, and do their best to help you eat the possum, or if you are attempting to lose weight, keep the BBQ possum from tempting you.

Finally, they will encourage you. Earlier, I mentioned the one who sees the best in you, and the encourager not only sees the best in you but also calls it out frequently in encouragement. They believe in you and in your ability, with God's help, to overcome your hard things.

They can see what you cannot see.

If you are trying to get healthy, tell them the possum in your life is your health. So, how does that look? Let's say you are ready to start exercising, and your goal is to walk three times a week for thirty minutes. You would find that supportive person and say, "My possum is a lack of exercise. I am going to start walking three times a week for thirty minutes each time. I need your support in my goal."

They may ask you why you are exercising or may even volunteer to join you in your goal. These are both important, because how you validate your reason for exercise is how you value exercise. If you say, "I am walking because it will help me to build stamina," then vocalize that you value stamina.

If you validate weight loss for a healthy lifestyle, then you will vocalize that you value being healthy. These validations provide you and your support friend with the reason you want to eat a possum.

Consider it your "motive to change."

These are legitimate reasons for change, but what about those other reasons? There are times we validate our reason for change and it may reveal an unhealthy view of ourselves or someone else. For example, you may validate your reason for weight loss by noting that you are doing it to get revenge because a love interest found love in another who did not struggle with weight issues. Your attempt to change may be an unhealthy view of your body image or, worse, may reveal deeper issues that have nothing to do with weight. A supportive person may hear your validation for "eating a possum" and may question your motives. This may well provide you with context for a deeper issue than losing weight may provide.

In the case of my literal moment of eating a possum, I had to determine whether I would do it to please others or if I really wanted to enjoy the culinary adventure heaped on a plate a few inches away. This is vital for you, because your motive is key to your success. The validation for eating the possum for me was to own up to a desire to please people for acceptance or to enter into the transactional mode of eating a possum because I wanted to taste and see if the possum was good. So, I validated my exercise of trying the possum by declaring that I was not doing it because everyone wanted me to eat it, but I was going to try it because I wanted to see what barbecued possum tasted like. I also declared that one bite would suffice if I found the taste offensive.

I had plenty of support for my encounter, but I needed to ensure that I was eating the possum for the right reason. The same is true for whatever you are attempting. Your success may be based on your validation of eating your possum (again, it will become what you value) and your support from friends and will become the foundation for future success.

If I need to get fit, and I have asked the Lord to help me, I need to tell someone so they can ask me how I'm doing with my hard thing, so they can support me while I battle my hard thing, and so I can be encouraged as I face my hard thing.

You've got to say, "My enemy surrounds me, and I can't do this alone." In 2 Kings 6, an enemy surrounded Elisha and his servant. The enemy was everywhere. It scared the servant so severely that he shared the hard things in his life with the prophet.

What are we going to do?

He was afraid.

"So," Elisha said, "Don't be afraid; those who are with us are more than those who are with them." What Elisha said didn't make sense if you are a math guy or a math girl. The servant may have gotten his hand out... and counted, "Me... Elisha... two vs. 100,000."

He may have thought that Elisha had been drinking the fire water. He may have thought: *"This is great! I am surrounded by an enemy bent on my destruction, and the one person with me has delusions of grandeur. He has delusions of delusions."*

But Elisha had eaten the possum before; he wasn't deluded. He was experienced. His words were only meant to encourage the servant, because he knew the Lord was on their side.

And Elisha prayed, "Open his eyes, Lord, so that he may see." Then the Lord opened the servant's eyes, and he looked and saw the hills full of horses and chariots of fire all around Elisha. As the enemy came down toward him, Elisha prayed to the Lord, "Strike this army with blindness." So, he struck them with blindness, as Elisha had asked. (2 Kings 6:17-18, NIV)

You need that kind of person with you when you face your hard thing, the one who has experienced the hard thing. You have told them your hard thing, and they encourage you to confront it and achieve victory over it.

Hebrews 10:24 says, "And let us consider how we may spur one another on toward love and good deeds."

They can also support your endeavor.

Paul wrote, "Carry each other's burdens, and in this way, you will fulfill the law of Christ" (Galatians 6:2).

They can also pray for your victory and hold you accountable.

This support is not only with people, but also with God. God is ready and able to help you overcome the most difficult things in your life. Joshua's final words to the Jewish people indicate a God who is active and able to help.

> "For the Lord has driven out great and powerful nations for you, and no one has yet been able to defeat you. Each one of you will put to flight a thousand of the enemy, for the Lord your God fights for you, just as he has promised. So be very careful to love the Lord your God." (Joshua 23:9-11)

An accountability agreement will help you on your journey. Here are two agreements that you can use to establish mutual trust and accountability (also available in the *Eat the Possum Workbook*).

TEMPLATE 1: GENERAL ACCOUNTABILITY PARTNERSHIP AGREEMENT

We, [Partner 1] and [Partner 2], agree to support each other in overcoming our respective challenges ("possums"). We commit to:

1. Meet/communicate [frequency, e.g., weekly] to discuss progress.
2. Be honest about our struggles and successes.
3. Offer encouragement and constructive feedback.
4. Maintain confidentiality about our discussions.
5. Help each other stay focused on our goals.
6. Celebrate milestones and achievements together.

Our specific "possums" and goals are:

[Partner 1's possum and goal]
[Partner 2's possum and goal]

Signed: _____ Date: _____
[Partner 1]
Signed: _____ Date: _____
[Partner 2]

TEMPLATE 2: SPECIFIC GOAL ACCOUNTABILITY CHECKLIST

Goal: [State specific goal, e.g., "Walk thirty minutes, three times a week."]

Week of: _____

Day	Completed?	Notes
Mon		
Tue		
Wed		
Thu		
Fri		
Sat		
Sun		

Challenges faced this week:

Strategies for improvement:

Accountability partner feedback:

TEMPLATE 3: MONTHLY PROGRESS REVIEW

Month: _____

1. What progress have you made towards eating your "possum" this month?

2. What obstacles did you encounter?

3. How did you overcome (or plan to overcome) these obstacles?

4. What support did you receive from your accountability partner?

5. What additional support do you need?

6. Goals for next month:

7. Accountability partner comments:

TEMPLATE 4: SUPPORT AND ENCOURAGEMENT LOG

Date: _____

Possum being addressed: _____

Today's challenge:

How I plan to tackle it:

Words of encouragement from my accountability partner:

Scripture or quote for motivation:

How I felt after discussing with my partner:

TEMPLATE 5: SPIRITUAL STRENGTH AND TRUTH-SPEAKING SESSION

Date: _____

Opening Prayer:

Scripture focus for today's session:

Truth spoken by accountability partner:

How this truth applies to my "possum":

Action steps based on this truth:

Closing encouragement and prayer:

This support, encouragement, and accountability are so key to your success. Those who are they who serve in this manner can provide you with what you need for the next step, and this step may be the hardest of all.

CHAPTER 8 QUESTIONS:

1. Who in your life embodies the qualities of a supportive accountability partner as described in the chapter? How can you approach them about supporting you in your "possum-eating" journey?
2. What is your specific "possum" (challenge) that you need to share with your chosen accountability partner? How can you clearly articulate your goal and the support you need?
3. Reflecting on the chapter's emphasis on validation, what is your true motive for tackling this challenge? How does this motive align with your values and long-term goals?
4. The chapter mentions potential negative reactions when sharing your goals. How can you prepare yourself mentally and emotionally for possible initial skepticism or opposition from others?
5. Which of the provided accountability agreement templates resonates most with your situation? How can you adapt it to best suit your needs and those of your accountability partner?
6. The chapter emphasizes the importance of spiritual support. How can you incorporate prayer or spiritual guidance into your accountability process?
7. Considering the story of Elisha and his servant, how can you cultivate a perspective that sees beyond immediate challenges to the greater support and resources available to you?

A SUMMARY OF CHAPTER 8 OF *EAT THE POSSUM*:

- Share your "possum" (challenge) with a trusted friend or accountability partner.
- Choose someone who:
  1. Sees your potential.
  2. Can speak truth in love.
  3. Has your best interests in mind.
  4. Provides support, accountability, and encouragement.
- Timing is crucial: Share your goal when you're prepared to embark on the journey with determination.
- Avoid unsupportive individuals who may sabotage your progress.
- Understand that accountability is not about policing, but about support and encouragement.
- Clearly communicate your goal and the specific support you need.
- Validate your reasons for change, as they reflect what you value.
- Examine your motives to ensure they're healthy and aligned with your true goals.
- Consider using accountability agreements or templates to structure your support system.
- Recognize the importance of both human and spiritual support in overcoming challenges.
- Be prepared for potential initial skepticism or opposition when sharing your goals.
- Remember that success often depends on having the right support system and validating your reasons for change.
- Utilize tools like accountability checklists, progress

reviews, and encouragement logs to track your journey.
- Incorporate spiritual strength and truth-speaking sessions if they are aligned with your beliefs.
- Reflect on the story of Elisha and his servant to cultivate a perspective that sees beyond immediate challenges.

CHAPTER NINE

TENDERIZING TOUGH POSSUM MEAT

A t this point, a warning is necessary: one of the most significant problems with problems is their tendency to grow if left alone. They seem to take on a life of their own and hinder any practical victory. Once we are confronted with problems, we must deal with them immediately, or they will become more pervasive in our minds than they really are. Also, they may set up a "hardness aversion" in us that hinders overcoming obstacles.

What is "hardness aversion?" *It is resistance to something that has become too difficult to overcome after repeated events that create extreme dislike, opposition, aversion, or antipathy.* This kind of sounds like a possum to me.

For example, you may have tried to overcome an addiction but were unsuccessful and, after various attempts to overcome it, resigned yourself to believe that it was too big for you to overcome. The problem may not have been as complex as it was in your mind. If you attempt and fail enough times, you will begin to believe you are a failure at everything, or at least you can never overcome the specific problem. Throughout history, individuals have faced insurmountable obstacles, but never gave up, and because they persevered, we have benefited. Thomas Edison failed 2,774 times to reach the working design of an electric light bulb. He had to persevere until he found the proper method for his experiment to work. Your problem may be due to hardness aversion more than the problem itself. If you believe that success is attainable once you have the right tools, you might just be able to experience victory by eating the possum. Think of the various tools that might make your possum manageable, for therein you may find success where you have never experienced it before.

Hardness aversion is an obstacle that may require a particular mindset change if it stands in the way of victory.

THE LONE SOLDIER'S DILEMMA

Paul urged Timothy to endure hardness as a good soldier (2 Timothy 2:3-5). But what if you're the one loading your own backpack with bricks? What if your exhaustion stems from trying to be a one-person army? What if your aversion to hardship is really just fatigue from lugging around a solo burden?

We often run out of steam when we're carrying more than our fair share. I've been there, huffing and puffing under a load that was never meant for one person. When we rely solely on our own muscle, we end up dragging a boulder uphill alone. No wonder we resist change—we're too busy catching our breath.

Some of us are worn to the bone, not because life's tough, but because we're playing lone wolf. Your personal fuel tank has a bottom. Your brain's hard drive has limited storage. Even wisdom comes with an expiration date.

Want to know the biggest lesson I took from my doctorate? I realized I know squat. Zip. Nada. The deeper I dug, the more questions popped up like whack-a-mole. Each answer birthed a litter of new puzzles (possums), leading me down rabbit holes of endless inquiry. Like a dog with a bone, I chased, I researched, I pondered, I chased some more. This wild goose chase taught me two things: first, my ignorance is vast, and second, there's a delicious mystery out there daring me to solve it.

The hunt for answers became a thrilling game, with the prize being the solution to my problem. But here's the kicker: trying to muscle through with just my own smarts was like bringing a spoon to a gunfight. The real magic happened when I did my part but let the God handle the heavy lifting. That's when success stopped playing hard to get.

That's the ugly truth: God *will* allow more than you can handle. He will not give you more temptation (1 Corinthians 10:13) than you can handle, but He will let you carry as much as you try to carry until you ask Him for help.

I learned this the hard way. I struggled and struggled, added more weight than my strength would permit, and wondered why God "allowed" me to have so much weight. He didn't! He allowed me to struggle until my pride gave way to surrender, and that surrender would mean that I could experience miracles He provided by carrying the load.

If I tried it on my own, I would miss the miracles. If I involved God, I would be witness to how God continually amazes His children with His infinite wisdom and power. I thought if I had large enough brains that it would matter, but I quickly learned that the contents were the least important thing, because God wasn't looking at the contents; He just wanted a vessel He could use. Trying hard enough alone is not enough to overcome.

That's why a lot of people have an aversion to hardness. They did some or all of it independently, wearing them out. They are tired of being tired. So, the next time a complex thing comes, they report AWOL (Absent without Leave).

Unfortunately, it's disheartening for those on the front lines of the battle to fight with their supporters running from hard things.

It emboldens the enemy when you walk away from the hard things. It is there that he finds your stress point. At that stress point, he overcomes you, overwhelms you, and instead of calling on God for help, you are tempted to walk away and give up. You want to stop trying, and the enemy of your soul wins by default.

People say, "It's hard living for Jesus." It *is* hard, but it is impossible to do it alone. We need God's help *and* one another to see victory.

If you are going to overcome the most challenging things in your life alone, you will reach a maximum limit. Your limit does not have to be your limitation.

Most people know their limits, but when those limits become limitations, they become the place where the excuses start.

Please don't stop reading. The limit lets you know where your ability ends, but it is the very place where God's power takes over.

I am living proof of this. In 2022, God challenged me to be challenged. I was in the middle of working on my doctorate and was pastoring a church in Indiana. I reached a place in my ministry life where I could pastor in my sleep. I was on autopilot. It was easy. I was swimming in the shallow end and not challenged at all.

For a follower of Jesus Christ, that is the most insidious place ever. If you can do everything you do for God without much effort, or no effort, you are doing something wrong.

God called me to do the hard thing.

At first, I thought the hard thing was to complete my doctorate. When I successfully defended my project, I was happy and content and celebrated overcoming this obstacle. For me, it was an amazing accomplishment. But God wanted me to stop treading water in the shallow end and follow Him by doing what He called me to do. That's when He led me to resign my pastorate and write. That church was a church I had planted in 2007, and the people had walked through a *lot* of challenging things with me and my family. This book is not long enough to detail the setbacks and miracles of that journey, but, honestly, I had reached a limit, and at first, it was okay.

Then, God told us to resign, sell most of our belongings, and move to Texas. We moved when the Texas heat was breaking records. It was like a cruel welcome when we arrived because it was so sweltering. We left jobs, friends, and more to go to an uncertain place with very few friends. It was hard, but the peace of God was there all along.

We all know we are limited, but we fail to consider that the devil is also restricted. He has limited power, limited ability, and limited authority. There was something that I experienced and still experience today: the grace of resilience.

I believe that resiliency helped us overcome hardness aversion. Oxford defines resiliency as "the capacity to withstand or to recover quickly from difficulties; toughness."[1]

The very thing that causes hardness aversion is too many setbacks from which one does not fully recover. Sometimes, the person fails to recover due to an inadequate support system, setting too high of an initial achievable goal, or spending too much time overthinking once the setback occurred. The ability to overcome the aversion then includes the opposite of those, including a reliable support system (which we have already noted in the types of friends needed to eat the possum); setting smaller achievable goals to increase confidence in achieving the hard goal; and changing *the way* you think, instead of merely *what* you think. We covered that in an earlier chapter.

Resilience also involves reframing your perspective, such as when we see a setback as failure. They are challenges that end in defeat or an insurmountable obstacle. I am reminded of my three-year-old grandson. When he had a goal of getting closer to the countertop to get a treat, he began trying to climb the cabinets to achieve his goal. It would end with tears and a little boy on his back, failing to obtain his goal. Eventually, however, he learned that the insurmountable object was merely a stepping-stone away from victory, so he moved a chair, step stool, box, or

---

1. https://www.oed.com/search/dictionary/?scope=Entries&q=resiliency

whatever that enabled his climb into the position of victory. He never gave up or announced defeat. He merely reframed his perspective and won the victory.

We must do the same. Even after multiple times of failures, we have to have a mindset that we have not achieved victory (x) a number of times, but it brought us one step closer to victory. We might have to move a chair, or a mindset, or even a goal, so that the greater goal was within reaching distance. If we give up, we will never taste the sweet barbecued delicacy; we will simply live defeated. The greater problem with that is that we sometimes start to feel that we can never win at *any*thing, so once we face a giant, we hide behind a rock, hoping it will go away on its own. It usually doesn't and will tell every other hard thing you are unwilling to engage. You become a slave, shipped off to failure land, never to win at anything big ever again.

Let today be the day you change that destiny.

I love the many Psalms, but the one that comes to mind is Psalm 23. In verse 5, David wrote, "You prepare a feast for me in the presence of my enemies. You honor me by anointing my head with oil. My cup overflows with blessings." I imagine the enemy having to watch as God prepares your feast to honor you while that same enemy seethes in anger. As you eat the possum, the enemy cannot stop God nor you. Learn resilience and shun aversion to hardness. Know that God is for you and longs to help you become victorious over the hard things that you are facing. Here are some additional Scriptures that speak to this:

Joshua 1:5,

> "No one will be able to stand against you as long as you live. For I will be with you as I was with Moses. I will not fail you or abandon you."

Josh 21:44-45,

> And the LORD gave them rest on every side, just as he had solemnly promised their ancestors. None of their enemies could stand against them, for the LORD helped them conquer all their enemies. Not a single one of all the good promises the LORD had given to the family of Israel was left unfulfilled; everything he had spoken came true.

How is this possible?

> Isaiah 40:31: "but they who wait for the Lord shall renew their strength; they shall mount up with wings like eagles; they shall run and not be weary; they shall walk and not faint" (English Standard Version).

> Isaiah 41:10: "fear not, for I am with you; be not dismayed, for I am your God; I will strengthen you, I will help you, I will uphold you with my righteous right hand" (ESV).

> Ephesians 3:16: "...that according to the riches of his glory he may grant you to be strengthened with power through his Spirit in your inner being" (ESV).

> Daniel 11:32: "And such as do wickedly against the covenant shall he corrupt by flatteries: but the people that do know their God shall be strong, and do exploits" (KJV).

I love the word "exploits," for it means an "act remarkable for brilliance, daring or bold deed!" For a follower of Jesus, it means to finish the challenge in such a way that the enemy does not know what hit him while others stand in awe.

God destined you to do exploits for Him, and once you begin to taste the sweet success that comes from overcoming the hard things, the easier the next hard thing will become. That's why hardness aversion must be overcome, for when you do, you have greatness in your future.

A great story in the Old Testament precedes David's famous victory over Goliath (1 Samuel 17). The taunts of Goliath had already debilitated the Israeli army before David's arrival. The entire army suffered from hardness aversion. No one was willing to face Goliath on the battlefield. King Saul was also resistant to the battle because facing Goliath was too hard. When David arrives, he tells King Saul that he can defeat the giant and recalls previous victories he experienced while tending to the sheep in Bethlehem. He told him that he had killed a lion and a bear before and that the giant was not greater than God.

David's journey to slaying lions and bears wasn't an overnight success. It likely began with hesitant attempts to ward off predators—shouting from a distance or lobbing stones while his heart raced. When he relied on God to overcome, then it set him up for the next challenge. Each encounter, though terrifying, slowly chipped away at his fear. As the beasts grew bolder, so did David's resolve, for he already knew that victory was possible with God. He pushed himself to confront the discomfort, inching closer to danger with each skirmish. These repeated face-offs with deadly predators, as he walked with God, forged his character in the crucible of fear and duty. David embraced the hardship, recognizing that each difficult encounter was a steppingstone to greater strength. Over time, his initial aversion to the heart-pounding, palm-sweating confrontations transformed into a steely determination. By consistently choosing to face the hard path—protecting his flock despite the danger—David cultivated the grit and resilience that would ultimately enable him to triumph over these formidable foes. He did *not* do this alone. He had God on his side, enabling David to experience victory.

This consistent exposure to danger and difficulty reshaped his mindset. By the time David stood before Goliath, he had cultivated a robust mental fortitude. His past victories over fear and hesitation and experience with God had forged an unshakeable confidence. David had learned to lean into hardship, trusting that God would equip him to overcome any challenge, no matter how daunting.

He was not reckless like his brothers thought; he was resilient.

That's precisely what victory over your hard thing offers: the ability to face more significant problems in the future because you have experience eating your possum. Your hard thing, or your possum, is not a roadblock, roadkill, or wall as much as a steppingstone. Victory there will encourage accomplishment everywhere else. Deal with your hard thing, and you will experience the good pleasure of God, and you will see remarkable success after victory.

When we overcome hardness aversion, we stand confidently before the enemy everyone else is afraid of. It's not because we are ignorant of the power of the enemy; it is because we have experienced the power of God over and over again until victory was complete.

Here are specific strategies for overcoming resistance to change or "hardness aversion":

1. Reframe Your Perspective
    - View setbacks as challenges rather than failures. Rather than failing, you are one step closer to success.
    - See obstacles as opportunities for growth and learning. Learn what you can so that you experience victory the next time.
    - Focus on the process and progress rather than just the end goal. Love to love the journey, not just the destination.
2. Set Smaller, Achievable Goals
    - Break down larger goals into smaller, manageable tasks.

- Celebrate small victories to build confidence and momentum. We will lean into this principle in a later chapter.
- Gradually increase the difficulty of goals as you progress.

3. Develop Resilience
    - Practice bouncing back from setbacks quickly.
    - Learn from failures and use them as steppingstones. Write down what you learned from the experience and allow it to teach you new things.
    - Cultivate a growth mindset that embraces challenges. Don't be afraid of the big things, but let them challenge you.

4. Leverage Your Support System
    - Rely on the supportive individuals identified in earlier chapters.
    - Share your struggles and successes with your accountability partners.
    - Ask for help and encouragement when facing difficult challenges. Remember, even the Lone Ranger had Tonto.

5. Change Your Thinking Patterns
    - Focus on changing how you think, not just what you think.
    - Challenge negative self-talk and replace it with positive affirmations. If you say things like, "I always make stupid choices," you will always make stupid choices. But if you say, "I learned _____from my experience," you will begin to see yourself differently.
    - Practice mindfulness to stay present and avoid overthinking

6. Embrace Discomfort

- Recognize that growth often comes from stepping out of your comfort zone.
- View discomfort as a sign of progress rather than a reason to quit.
- Gradually expose yourself to challenging situations to build tolerance.

7. Learn from Others' Experiences
   - Study examples of people who have overcome similar challenges
   - Seek advice and mentorship from those who have succeeded in areas you struggle with.
   - Draw inspiration from stories of perseverance and resilience.
8. Focus on Your "Why"
   - Regularly remind yourself of the reasons behind your goals.
   - Connect your current challenges to your larger life purpose.
   - Use visualization techniques to imagine the benefits of overcoming your "possum."
9. Practice Self-Compassion
   - Be kind to yourself when facing setbacks.
   - Recognize that everyone struggles with change and difficult tasks.
   - Allow yourself room for mistakes and learning.
10. Take Immediate Action
    - Combat procrastination by taking small, immediate steps towards your goal.
    - Use the 30-second rule mentioned earlier to act on your intentions quickly.
    - Build momentum through consistent, daily actions.

CHAPTER 9 QUESTIONS:

1. Reflect on a time when you experienced "hardness aversion" in your life. How did it manifest, and what were the consequences of avoiding the challenge?
2. The chapter mentions that problems tend to grow if left alone. Can you identify a current challenge in your life that might be getting worse due to avoidance? How can you address it promptly?
3. How can you apply the concept of "the grace of resilience" to a difficult situation you're currently facing? What small, achievable goals can you set to build confidence and momentum?
4. The chapter discusses reframing setbacks as steppingstones. Think of a recent failure or setback. How can you reframe it as a learning opportunity or a step towards eventual success?
5. Considering the story of David and Goliath, how can you use past experiences of overcoming smaller challenges to build confidence in tackling larger obstacles in your life?
6. The chapter emphasizes the importance of relying on God and others rather than trying to overcome challenges alone. Who in your life can you reach out to for support in your current "possum-eating" journey?
7. Review the specific strategies for overcoming resistance to change listed at the end of the chapter. Which one resonates most with you, and how can you implement it in your life this week?

A SUMMARY OF CHAPTER 9 OF *EAT THE POSSUM*:

- Problems tend to grow if left unaddressed, potentially leading to "hardness aversion."
- Hardness aversion is resistance to difficult tasks due to repeated failures or negative experiences.
- Overcoming hardness aversion often requires a mindset change and perseverance.
- Trying to overcome challenges alone can lead to exhaustion and discouragement.
- Involving God and others in your struggles can lead to experiencing miracles and overcoming seemingly insurmountable obstacles.
- Resilience is key to overcoming hardness aversion, defined as the capacity to withstand or recover quickly from difficulties.
- Reframing perspective is crucial: view setbacks as challenges rather than failures.
- Setting smaller, achievable goals can build confidence and momentum towards larger objectives.
- A support system is vital for overcoming difficult challenges.
- Embracing discomfort and viewing it as a sign of progress rather than as a reason to quit is important.
- Taking immediate action and combating procrastination can help build momentum.
- The chapter uses biblical references to illustrate the importance of relying on God's strength and promises.
- The story of David and Goliath is used to demonstrate how overcoming smaller challenges can prepare you for larger ones.
- Overcoming hardness aversion can lead to greater

achievements and the ability to face more significant challenges in the future.
- The chapter provides specific strategies for overcoming resistance to change, including reframing perspective, developing resilience, and leveraging support systems.

CHAPTER TEN

POSSUM PARTY: TOASTING YOUR TRIUMPH

The next principle is powerful. It remembers former victories in light of the present struggles. Many people are afraid to face their Goliaths because they fail to remember the smaller victories God made through them. David did not. When the time came for David to face Goliath, his brothers called him "foolish," but David was anything but foolish. They taunted him that he was just a weak, impetuous brother who was going to get killed. But David recalled the times he defeated lions and bears who were trying to kill the sheep. He remembered a previous victory, which gave him leverage for future engagements (1 Samuel 17:34). This is vital to your possum eating. Remembering all the times you won will help you confidently face your next battle.

David was a boy, probably in his mid-teens, when he faced Goliath. While we don't know his age when he faced the lion or bear, we know that he was successful and recalled it to those who questioned his ability. But what gave him the courage to face the lion or bear? It may have been the "spirit of fed up" that was mentioned earlier. It could have been other situations where David recalled previous victories over snakes and when he chased off the lion or bear (before he killed them). In other words, there were probably a lot of small victories that led up to and leveraged the big win.

I am not minimizing the power of God to overcome Goliath, nor do I believe David won the victory himself. Instead, he had experience with the God of the impossible, for David had experienced God's power repeatedly. When we remember the victories God wrought on our behalf, we can experience greater victories because we know what God is capable of doing. I don't believe David showed up unprepared for the battle, and he was experienced in faith to believe that God would give him victory, as God had done multiple times in David's life.

I can personally testify to this powerful principle. I was fifteen and decided to train for a race in Little Rock, Arkansas. It was a 10K race where people worldwide were invited to participate, and the winner received a great prize. In my recollection, it was a cash prize, because, as a teenager without a car, I would do anything I could to raise money to buy a decent car. And so I ran.

The race was held in September, so I trained all summer long for it. Unfortunately, this particular summer was the hottest in Arkansas history. The temperature hit over one hundred degrees for over thirty days straight, with lows in the upper eighties for most of that time. I trained in the morning and the evening, running between three and mile miles each time. The fatigue due to the heat was overwhelming, as was dehydration and possible heat stroke, but I trained nonetheless.

The physical toll was not the only battle; I did not expect the mental toll. It was hard to continue to train when every fiber of my body screamed for relief.

When my body reached its limit, I learned a lesson in mental perseverance. As I ran, I focused on the next mailbox and thought, *John, if you can make it to the next mailbox, you can stop.*

So, I ran with the purpose of getting to the next mailbox and made it.

Then I thought, *John, you did it! Now, try to make it to the next mailbox*. I made it and continued this thinking, using my "next mailbox philosophy" ™ to encourage the next part of my training. I used the small victories to lead me to greater victories.

This is so important to your possum eating (or hard thing). You have likely faced hard things before. You have experienced small victories and likely missed their potential impact on future battles. If you know the Lord, you have likely faced a lot of battles and won them with His help. You have persevered and know victory.

So, take a moment and think about a previous battle you have won. If your possum is a desire to lose weight, think of the times you lost weight, even if it was a pound.

If your possum is a struggling marriage, remember the relationship victories you have experienced with your spouse.

If it is in becoming debt-free, remember the times you were able to pay off a small bill.

Those small victories can become leverage in the big battle. They are encouragement that God can help you overcome, because He has done so in the past.

Think about all the feasts and festivals God instituted for the Jewish people. They all commemorated some type of battle, struggle, and journey where God gave them a great victory. They were not just designed to provide thankfulness or use as a memorial for God's work in the past, but to encourage the people to believe in Him to work for them in the present. It served both purposes, and when Jesus arrived, He made a connection between past events and His presence on Earth.

They were designed to leverage the people's minds to the awesomeness of God. Your victories with God should do the same.

Many of the Jews didn't get it, but, after the resurrection, the apostles leveraged all they had learned to call the dead back to life, to tell a lame man to walk again, and to praise their way out of prison.

Your past victory is not only meant for thankfulness (which

is very important) but also to use as leverage for your future victory. God can and will do it again.

Don't miss this connection, and don't get discouraged.

We want instant success when we are challenged with our possum. We want to lose fifty pounds instantly instead of celebrating the small victories. We want instant happiness in our marriage instead of celebrating great singular moments. We want a winning lottery ticket without taking time to trudge along paying off small bills. If we celebrate small victories and leverage them for future success while keeping our eyes on Jesus, we will see even greater victories.

That is the key.

When the plate of barbecued possum was placed in front of me, I had to remember previous moments of victories over distasteful things to encourage the moment.

This will sound wild, but during that extremely hot summer training for the race, I returned home after an evening run. I was hot, needing relief from the heat, and incredibly hungry. My mom was cooking something that smelled amazing. I told her that I wanted everything in the skillet she was frying. I even said, "I want all of it." She laughed and said, "Well then, what will I cook for everyone else?" I said, "Whatever you have to cook, I just want that awesome fried food from heaven for myself."

She laughed, and I took a shower to cool down.

When I finished my shower, Mom called out, "Your skillet full of fried food from heaven awaits you; hurry before it gets cold."

I sat down, devoured every bit of it, and asked, "Okay, what did I just eat?" My mom laughed because it was something that I had previously hated. But in this one instance, I loved it. In fact, that fried food became my "go-to" birthday celebration dinner. If you think it was "fried possum," you would be wrong; it was fried chicken livers.

When I sat down at the table with the barbecued possum

plate in front of me, I remembered that the most distasteful thing does not have to be *the thing* that keeps you from victory. If you face it, eat it; you might just like it. Who knows? You might just love it.

Celebrating small victories is helpful for every area of our lives, but, honestly, at least we should be thankful for them. Mostly, if you are like me, I forget them. I can't tell you the number of times I have struggled over things I previously experienced victory over. It was because I forgot about it. The element of thankfulness keeps those small victories in our minds.

Here are some additional concrete strategies for celebrating and leveraging small wins, along with a section on creating a "victory journal" and scientific research on the benefits of celebrating achievements.

CONCRETE STRATEGIES FOR CELEBRATING AND LEVERAGING SMALL WINS:

1. Create a "Win Wall" by designating a space in your home or office to display the accomplishments you've made visually. Use Post-it notes, photos, or small mementos to represent each win.
2. Implement a "Three Wins" daily practice: At the end of each day, write down three things you accomplished, no matter how small. That's why making up your bed is a great start to the day; it gives you a sense of immediate accomplishment.
3. Share your wins with an accountability partner: Schedule regular check-ins to discuss progress and celebrate together.
4. Reward system: Set up a tiered reward system for different levels of achievements. For example, small wins might earn you a favorite healthy snack, while bigger wins could merit a night out.

5. Progress tracking app: Visually represent your progress and celebrate streaks of consistency using a habit-tracking app.

CREATING A VICTORY JOURNAL (OR USE THE *EAT THE POSSUM VICTORY JOURNAL*):

A victory journal is a powerful tool for documenting and reflecting on your achievements. Here's how to create one:

1. Choose your medium: This could be a physical notebook, a digital document, or a specialized journaling app.
2. Set a regular schedule: Commit to writing in your journal daily or weekly.
3. Structure your entries: Include the date, the achievement, how you felt about it, and what you learned from the experience.
4. Be specific: Instead of vague statements, use concrete details. For example, "I ran for twenty minutes without stopping," instead of, "I exercised."
5. Reflect on patterns: Periodically review your journal to identify trends in your achievements and areas for growth.
6. Include setbacks: Document how you overcame challenges, as these are also victories.
7. Add visual elements: Include photos, drawings, or other visual representations of your achievements.

WHY IS IT IMPORTANT TO CELEBRATE?

Alright, possum eaters, let's talk about why celebrating your wins is more than just patting yourself on the back—it's like adding secret sauce to your possum-eating skills! You know how that first bite of barbecued possum tastes like victory? Well, science says that feeling isn't just in your taste buds—it's rewiring your brain for more wins!

MOTIVATION BOOST

Remember when you finally took that first bite of possum? It turns out that savoring that moment does more than just make you feel good. Some smart folks in lab coats discovered that celebrating small wins lights a fire under you to keep going after bigger possums. So next time you conquer a challenge, no matter how small, give yourself a high five; you're actually fueling up for the next battle!

HAPPY POSSUM, HAPPY LIFE

But, wait, there's more! Celebrating isn't just about pumping yourself up for the next possum. Research shows that folks who take time to enjoy their victories are just plain happier in life. It's like each celebration adds a little more seasoning to your overall life satisfaction. So go ahead, do a victory dance after each possum eaten. You're not just being silly; you're seasoning your life!

BELIEVE IN YOUR POSSUM-EATING POWERS

Here's where it gets really interesting. Every time you celebrate a win, you're actually convincing yourself that you're a bona fide possum-eater extraordinaire. And guess what? That belief makes you even better at tackling the next possum that comes your way. It's like a superpower that grows stronger each time you use it! That does not discount the power of God. It enhances our confidence in God working in our life, helping us overcome every obstacle.

STRESS-BUSTING CELEBRATION

Life's full of stress, right? Well, here's a tasty remedy: celebrate more! Scientists found out that taking time to enjoy your achievements, even the little ones, can melt away stress faster than possum fat on a hot grill. So next time life's got you feeling overwhelmed, remember your wins and let that celebration work its stress-busting magic.

YOUR BRAIN ON CELEBRATION

Now, here's the really cool part. When you celebrate, your brain throws a little party of its own. It releases this feel-good chemical called dopamine, which is like your brain's way of saying, "Hey, that was awesome! Let's do more of that!" It's nature's way of encouraging you to keep eating those possums and conquering those challenges.

So, possum eaters, remember this: every time you celebrate a win, you're not just having a good time. You're motivating yourself, boosting your happiness, building your confidence, fighting stress, and literally rewiring your brain for more success. It's like a secret weapon in your possum-eating arsenal.

As we wrap up this possum-eating journey, remember that every step forward, every obstacle jumped, and every goal crushed deserves a moment in the spotlight. By celebrating these moments, you're not just patting yourself on the back—you're setting yourself up for even bigger, tastier possum-eating adventures ahead. So, fire up that grill, and let's celebrate your possum-eating prowess!

By implementing these strategies, creating a victory journal, and understanding the scientific benefits of celebration, you can more effectively leverage your small wins to build momentum towards overcoming your biggest challenges.

What victory have you overcome recently? It doesn't even have to relate to your possum. It could be completely unrelated.

It could be an easy victory, or a hard one. For example, maybe you have recently finished reading a novel. It was a victory. Maybe it was not an incredible 358-page novel by J.W. Utley (*Meeting Jack Cash*), but a book of the Bible, or even a chapter. Celebrate the win. Recently, I shared with a group of friends that I was reading the Bible through this year, like I have done over and over again through the years. One remarked, "I could never do that. It's just too hard."

I told them that I read about ten to fifteen minutes a day from the Bible, and in a year, I will have read through the entire Old and New Testaments. They were surprised that it was merely a ten to fifteen minute a day exercise. Then I challenged them to pick a book of the New Testament and read a chapter a day for thirty days. If they did that, they would have read *at least* one New Testament book.

Even if they started with a paragraph at a time, I encouraged them to do *something*. Get a victory. Celebrate a win. That victory has a way of encouraging future endeavors.

CHAPTER 10 QUESTIONS:

1. Reflecting on David's experience with Goliath, what past victories in your life can you recall building confidence for your current challenges?
2. How can the author's "next mailbox" philosophy help you break down large goals into smaller, manageable steps?
3. Think about a recent small victory in your life. How can you leverage this success to tackle bigger challenges in your "possum-eating" journey?
4. The chapter emphasizes the importance of celebrating small wins. What specific strategies can you implement to acknowledge and celebrate your progress regularly, no matter how small?

5. Consider creating a victory journal, as mentioned in the chapter. How might this practice of documenting your achievements impact your motivation and perseverance?
6. The author discusses the scientific benefits of celebrating achievements, such as increased motivation and improved well-being. How can you incorporate this knowledge into your daily routine to enhance your personal growth?
7. Reflecting on the Jewish feasts and festivals mentioned in the chapter, how can you create personal celebrations or rituals to commemorate your victories and reinforce your faith in future success?

A SUMMARY OF CHAPTER 10 OF *EAT THE POSSUM*:

- Remembering past victories is crucial when facing new challenges.
- David's confidence in facing Goliath came from recalling his victories over lions and bears.
- Small victories can lead to and leverage bigger wins.
- The author's personal experience of training for a 10K race in extreme heat illustrates the power of perseverance. The "next mailbox" philosophy helps break down large goals into manageable steps.
- Recalling past successes can provide encouragement and leverage for current struggles.
- God's feasts and festivals for the Jewish people served as reminders of His past victories and encouragement for future challenges.
- Celebrating small victories is essential, rather than expecting instant success.
- The author's experience with fried chicken livers

demonstrates that overcoming initial aversions can lead to unexpected positive outcomes.
- Concrete strategies for celebrating small wins include:
  1. Creating a "Win Wall."
  2. Implementing a "Three Wins" daily practice.
  3. Sharing achievements with an accountability partner.
  4. Setting up a reward system.
  5. Using progress tracking apps.
- Creating a victory journal can help document and reflect on achievements.
- Scientific research supports the benefits of celebrating achievements, including:
  1. Increased motivation.
  2. Improved well-being.
  3. Enhanced self-efficacy.
  4. Stress reduction.
  5. Neurological benefits.
- Even small, unrelated victories can be leveraged for tackling bigger challenges.
- Consistent small efforts, like reading the Bible for ten to fifteen minutes daily, can lead to significant accomplishments over time.

CHAPTER ELEVEN
RIDING THE POSSUM WAVE

After you remember the victories in your past for your present problems, that is not where you stop. So, what happens when you have a victory? You celebrate, take a break, take a nap, stop?

You cannot stay in that mindset that says, *I ate the possum. Now I am going to take a nap.* You can't take a deep breath and let your guard down. You can't let the victory become a once-and-done kind of thing.

The greatest danger after a victory is taking the victory lap and feeling as if the battle is over. For one, the battle is not over when a victory is won, and two, that moment can hinder momentum.

That happened at the church I pastored a few years ago. The church had been hyper-mobile for four years. The church met in eleven different locations during that time, and we finally secured a lease on a building that would be a permanent location for another two years. There would be no need to send out monthly informational postcards advising people where we would be meeting, no need to set up and tear down equipment every week. The people were so excited to have a permanent home, but then something unforeseen happened. Everyone took a deep breath and became satisfied that we finally found a home. I later termed it the "great exhale." It was the moment when the people finally felt the church had arrived, and the people sat down. They stopped inviting people, they stopped serving, and they stopped attending groups. In their mind, the church had arrived, and they could take a break. It was the worst thing that had happened to the church, and something that looked like a victory actually worked against the church, because the leader failed to use the momentum. In reality, it was a victory, but the response of the people was to let down their guard and their desire to leverage this to the next goal.

They ate the possum and were satisfied. They won, took a victory lap, and then took a two-year nap.

The same thing can happen after you experience a significant victory. You can feel that you have arrived and then lose the best thing that can happen after a victory: *momentum*. And, believe me, momentum can be your very best friend.

For example, you can lose the twenty pounds that you have worked so hard to achieve and then take a victory lap and indulge in a celebratory meal. In no time, the victory was overwhelmed by the pounds that found their way back with a few extra friends.

Or you may eat a possum and restore a relationship. Forgiveness is extended and received, and you find a good place. Unfortunately, the relationship may revert to stagnation if there is no intentional focus on rebuilding it. Victory laps are good for the moment, but the future suffers from a lack of focus when one does not take the momentum to build for future success. Success doesn't automatically breed success, and momentum is not guaranteed in a vacuum. The best place to find momentum is right after a victory.

When you experience victory, the moments after providing a reason to celebrate, but they also contain amazing amounts of energy that may be used for the next battle.

In other words, momentum has proportional potential.

This is vital to overcoming hard things. It's almost like posting a sign on your heart that says to all possums: *if you come here, you will go down, and when you do, I will slap barbecue sauce on you and eat you.*

Momentum is best defined as:

"The amount of force a moving body has because of its weight and the speed at which it moves."

Momentum works the same whether you're a short person or a hefty one.

If you try to move a big rock, it will not travel very fast until you push it on a downhill slope—then watch out.

MOMENTUM IS A MOVING FORCE THAT OVERCOMES RESISTANCE.

We have talked about the story of David and Goliath already. We talked about David's confidence in victory because he had won other victories. He defeated the lion and the bear. I am sure when he clubbed them to death, it was after he had other encounters with them.

Once you win, you must look for the other battles to overcome. I am not talking about picking a fight, but be aware that following a victory will be a greater challenge. I used to be bothered by it, but now I am coming to expect it.

Momentum also works against us if not used immediately. The story of Elijah is a case in point. God told him that the rain would stop for three and one-half years. He prayed, and the rain stopped. Then God told Elijah to pray, and the rain started again. He told Elijah to confront the prophets of Baal. He did so, and on Mt. Carmel, he prayed fire down from heaven and consumed the sacrifice on the altar.

Immediately after those two powerful miracles occurred. He prayed, and rain came in a torrential downpour, and he outran King Ahab's chariot from Mt. Carmel to Jezreel. Each victory was followed by incredible momentum for the next battle. He had momentum, and he had God on his side. Unfortunately, in one instant, he lost momentum when Jezebel threatened to kill him. He ran for his life, deeply discouraged. He hid in a cave, and God had to use three different things to get his attention before He spoke to Elijah. Don't miss the moment of momentum, because when we lose it, we may forget all that God has already done for us.

I have known people with incredible talents and amazing victories who quickly decline emotionally when confronted with their next possum. They fail to utilize their momentum for the next thing.

On the contrary, I have also seen great victories give way to even greater ones when people found success and leveraged that for future movements. Once the stone begins its roll down the hill, it will gain speed and power. The same is true for our spiritual life.

I believe that is why David ran to meet Goliath. 1 Samuel 17:48-49 in the New Living Translation says:

> As Goliath moved closer to attack, David quickly ran out to meet him. Reaching into his shepherd's bag and taking out a stone, he hurled it with his sling and hit the Philistine in the forehead. The stone sank in, and Goliath stumbled and fell face down on the ground.

Let that sink in (not the stone, but the urgency): when David fought Goliath, he ran *towards* him. He used the momentum of previous victories to help him overcome the enemy, and then David ran to him. He ran *to* the battle.

Imagine the greatest battle in your life, but you have a rock rolling down a hill because you know the God you serve.

Some of you will say, "Sign me up for that! But you have to eat a possum first.

Then, you've got to get the BIG MO...

SEVEN KEYS TO MOMENTUM.

Harold Herring lists seven keys to getting momentum[1].

1. STOP SEEING YOURSELF THE WAY OTHERS SEE YOU.

We exercise our faith when we're confident of who we are in Christ. When we know our cause is just, and our calling is right, we should never be moved by what others, including friends and family members, may say. David could have listened to the naysayers, and one giant would have defeated the people of Israel (1 Samuel 17:28).

1 Samuel 17:28 in the New Living Translation says:

> But when David's oldest brother, Eliab, heard David talking to the men, he was angry. "What are you doing around here anyway?" he demanded. "What about those few sheep you're supposed to be taking care of? I know about your pride and deceit. You just want to see the battle!"

David's brother questioned his judgment, demeaned his work, and judged his motives without ever allowing him to respond.

You may have family or friends who view you and your goals the same way, but follow the wisdom of David as a young man.

1 Samuel 17:29-30 says:

> "And David said, 'What have I now done? Is there not a cause?' And he turned from him toward another, and spake after the same manner: and the people answered him again after the former manner."

---

1. Harold Herring, "7 Keys to Momentum," Rich Thoughts (blog), accessed August 8, 2024, https://haroldherring.com/blogs/harolds-blogs/richthoughts/846-7-keys-to-momentum.

David didn't defend himself. He merely asked if this wasn't a cause his brother believed in, and, without waiting for an answer, he turned and started talking with someone else.

To gain momentum in our lives, we need confidence in who we are in Christ and then turn our view toward the future.

And the last thing we need is the jealous or biased opinion of someone whose perspective limits their own reality and possibilities for the future.

2. DO NOT DESPISE SMALL BEGINNINGS

1 Samuel 17:40 in the Amplified Bible says:

> "Then he took his staff in his hand and chose five smooth stones out of the brook and put them in his shepherd's [lunch] bag [a whole kid's skin slung from his shoulder], in his pouch, and his sling was in his hand, and he drew near the Philistine."

Have you ever thought about what the Israelites and the Philistines were thinking when David reached down, picked up the five stones, and put them in his lunch sack?

The Israelites were probably saying, "Rocks—really? Is that kid going to fight the giant with rocks? We're in big trouble; we're probably all going to die here today."

The Philistines were probably snickering, laughing, and anticipating a great victory.

But what seemed small and insignificant to almost everybody else became a destiny changer in the hands of David.

The first job you ever had was just that: the first one. It didn't mean that your future success was stuck there. Don't let your life get stuck there. Your last failure was just that—your last failure. It was not your destiny.

Don't define your life by a single event or failure.

Walt Disney was fired from his first job for not being creative enough. J. K. Rowling was fired from a secretarial job because she spent too much time daydreaming about a boy... named Harry Potter.

A Baltimore television producer told Oprah Winfrey she was "unfit for the evening news." Have you ever heard of Handy Dan? It's the home-improvement chain that fired Bernie Marcus and Arthur Blank, which gave them the motivation to start Home Depot.

The list could go on! Never let anyone demean your ideas or minimize your potential for success. God planted the seeds in you, so don't let others dictate their fruit.

Zechariah 4:10 says:

> "Do not despise these small beginnings, for the Lord rejoices to see the work begin" "

It's not where you start in life, it's where you end up.

Our momentum, once started, will become an irresistible force regardless of how we began or where we are in life.

3. MAKE THE MOST OF WHERE YOU'RE AT AND WHAT YOU'RE DOING AT THE MOMENT.

When the Prophet Samuel came to Jesse's house to anoint the next king of Israel, David was not even considered. He was left out in the wilderness with the sheep (1 Samuel 16:22). Some people would have felt left out and offended because they weren't invited to meet the prophet. David was not. He was too busy fighting a lion and a bear with God's help.

But David made the most of where he was called to be, which gave him confidence when the opportunity arose before him.

1 Samuel 17:34-36 says:

> And David said unto Saul, "Thy servant kept his father's sheep, and there came a lion, and a bear, and took a lamb out of the

flock: And I went out after him, and smote him, and delivered it out of his mouth: and when he arose against me, I caught him by his beard, and smote him, and slew him. Thy servant slew both the lion and the bear: and this uncircumcised Philistine shall be as one of them, seeing he hath defied the armies of the living God."

If God has given you a big vision, but you don't yet see its manifestation, be diligent where you are and, by your faithfulness today, create momentum for your future.

Ask yourself what you can do at this very moment to improve where you're at.

Is there a self-study course you can take that will improve your performance on your job or that will contribute to your greater success in life?

Is there someone who's at or has been where you want to go in life? Who can serve as a mentor to you?

Are there habits that you need to cultivate or change that will increase your value in life and the marketplace?

Are you not sure? Ask God! He's happy to reveal what you need to do and when you need to do it.

Psalm 32:8 in the Amplified Bible says:

"I [the Lord] will instruct you and teach you in the way you should go; I will counsel you with My eye upon you."

You don't need to be like anyone else. You are an original. Just be and do what God created you to be and do.

4. IGNORE THE CRITICISMS OF OTHERS WHEN YOUR CAUSE IS JUST AND YOUR DIRECTION IS CLEAR.

Not only did David have to endure the ridicule and verbal abuse of his older brother, Eliab, which we discussed earlier, but he also had to deal with the doubt of King Saul.

1 Samuel 17:33 says:

"And Saul said to David, 'Thou art not able to go against this Philistine to fight with him: for thou art but a youth, and he a man of war from his youth.'"

If we allow the enemy or anyone else to make us question our age, whether young or old, our education, our experience, or the lack thereof, we will lose momentum.

Never allow anyone or anything other than the Word of God to determine your worth, value, or potential.

Sometimes, the most painful examination you'll ever receive is that from yourself, a close friend, or a mentor.

If you're employed, ask yourself these questions, and, yes, answer them honestly.

"If I were the boss, would I hire me?"

"If I were the boss, would I promote myself based on my job performance and attitude?"

"If I were the boss, would I give me a raise?"

Now, more importantly, ask God whether He would hire, promote, or give you a raise.

Colossians 3:23 in the Amplified Bible says:

"Whatever may be your task, work at it heartily (from the soul),
as [something done] for the Lord and not for men."

Sadly, many believers are not promoted or achieve their dreams because they are not faithful to where they are at the moment.

Never let a grumpy boss, a sarcastic supervisor, a lack of pay, or recognition keep you from doing the best job you can wherever you're assigned at the moment.

It's important, imperative, essential, absolutely necessary that we give our best efforts where we are regardless of what others say or do.

We can't control what other people say or do, but we can control how we act and react to what they do.

5. BECOME GOAL, REWARD MOTIVATED.

1 Samuel 17:24-26 says:

> "And all the men of Israel, when they saw the man, fled from him, and were sore afraid."

It's important to note that this verse says that "all the men of Israel," including David, ran from Goliath and were afraid.

But in reading 1 Samuel 17:25, we see where things changed for David, and he became goal... reward motivated.

> And the men of Israel said, "Have ye seen this man that is come up? Surely to defy Israel is he come up: and it shall be, that the man who killeth him, the king will enrich him with great riches, and will give him his daughter, and make his father's house free in Israel."

After running away from him, some of the men of Israel started talking about the reward being offered for killing Goliath.

But then something happened to change David's mind about the challenge. He had a defining moment based on new information and motivation.

David discovered that the person who killed Goliath would be given three things:

First, the warrior who defeated Goliath would receive "great riches." God has a benefit delivery system designed for every person who ever drew a breath on planet Earth. He desires for you to be rich, and that's why He gave you the power to get wealth (Deuteronomy 8:18).

Make no mistake: your enemy wants you broke, busted, and disgusted.

Once you realize who's fighting against you and the weapons available to you, you can begin your active pursuit of the prosperity God has for you. And that would give Him more pleasure than you realizing and manifesting what He intended for you to have (Psalm 35:27).

Second, the warrior, now victorious and wealthy, would receive the hand of the king's beautiful daughter in marriage.

When you marry into the king's family, you're immediately given a favored place in the court and opportunities for wealth and success beyond your previous experience or expectation.

Third, the victorious warrior would also have all their bills paid in full.

The enemy wants to keep you up to your eyeballs in debt, strung out by payments and with little, if any, hope of ever becoming debt-free.

The enemy wants you to believe that where you are in life right now is where you're going to stay. That's simply not true.

Upon learning of the reward, David made a profound statement in 1 Samuel 17:26 when he said:

> "'... who is this uncircumcised Philistine, that he should defy the armies of the living God?'"

David finally received the right motivation. What is your motivation?

Have you identified the motivation or reward you need to create your momentum for success?

6. RECOGNIZE WHO WILL FIGHT YOUR BATTLES

1 Samuel 17:44 says:

> "And the Philistine said to David, 'Come to me, and I will give thy flesh unto the fowls of the air, and to the beasts of the field.'"

The enemy, like a roaring lion, will seek to break your momentum by whatever methods he can, including fear of failure and of the unknown.

Let's look at four key verses of the forty-four verses found in the King James Bible, which instruct us to "be not afraid."

> *"... be not afraid of him..."* 2 Kings 1:15

> *"... be not afraid of them: for the LORD thy God is with thee..."* Deuteronomy 20:1

> *"... Thus saith the LORD unto you, Be not afraid nor dismayed by reason of this great multitude; for the battle is not yours, but God's."* 2 Chronicles 20:15

> *"... Be not afraid, only believe."* Mark 5:36.

These four verses tell us not to be afraid of "him" or "them" but to "only believe."

With God on our side, we have no reason to be afraid.
Psalm 118:6

> "'God's now at my side and I'm not afraid; who would dare lay a hand on me?'"

While the situations and problems we face on a daily basis may not be life and death, they are most often the choice between success or failure, mediocrity or excellence, malaise or momentum.

The momentum difference begins with the words of our mouth.

1 Samuel 17:45 says:

> "Then David said to the Philistine, "You come to me with a sword and with a spear and with a javelin, but I come to you in the name of the Lord of hosts, the God of the armies of Israel, whom you have defied" (ESV).

When you refuse to allow fear to break your momentum, when you know who you are in Him, then you will have a boldness in speaking to the giants in your life.

1 Samuel 17:46 says:

> "This day the Lord will deliver you into my hand, and I will strike you down and cut off your head. And I will give the dead bodies of the host of the Philistines this day to the birds of the air and to the wild beasts of the earth, that all the earth may know that there is a God in Israel" (ESV).

Who gave David the victory? "The Lord will deliver thee into mine hand."

In reading 1 Samuel 17:47, we clearly see David knew where his victory came from.

> "...and that all this assembly may know that the Lord saves not with sword and spear. For the battle is the Lord's, and he will give you into our hand" (ESV).

David ran to his giant with his mouth open with unstoppable spiritual momentum as Goliath fatally discovered.

Your momentum can't be stopped unless you allow it to happen.
When we do our part, God will do His part.
Zechariah 4:6 says:

"Not by might, nor by power, but by my spirit, saith the Lord of hosts" (KJV).

Every believer who uses principles based on the Word... will be energized, enlightened, and empowered by the Holy Spirit.
Can't think of a better way to create momentum for good than by obeying the voice of the Spirit?

7. CREATE A MOMENTUM FOR VICTORY

1 Samuel 17:48-49 in the Amplified Bible says:

"When the Philistine came forward to meet David, David ran quickly toward the battle line to meet the Philistine. David put his hand into his bag and took out a stone and slung it, and it struck the Philistine, sinking into his forehead, and he fell on his face to the earth."

You must be ready when the enemy shows up to break your momentum and kill your dreams.
The scripture says, "David ran quickly toward the battle line."
Don't be overly pensive or hesitant when facing a hard decision or a difficult problem to solve.
Aggressively pursue your dream; don't let anyone slow your momentum or create fear of failure.
Don't delay what needs to be done; do it now.
The scripture also says that David reached into his bag to grab the stones... he was prepared.

Preparation creates confidence, which produces momentum.

There is another surefire way to create momentum as a born-again child of God.

Revelation 2:11 in the Amplified Bible says:

> "And they overcame him by the blood of the Lamb [being born again], and by the word of their testimony [the words that come out of our mouths]; and they loved not their lives unto the death."

You can prevent the enemy from blocking or slowing your momentum by the blood of Jesus and through the words of your testimony.

As your journey to the debt-free lifestyle and the good life picks up momentum, praise God every step of the way for the mighty things He has allowed and empowered you to achieve.

The decision to create momentum in your life is yours; it will be created and as effective as you decide for it to be.

The effectiveness of your momentum will be determined by you and no one else.

Can this leverage be tailored to your specific personality type? The following suggestions might help you leverage your own type for momentum in the future:

ANALYTICAL ALEX (THINKER)

Alex can leverage victories by:

- Breaking down successful outcomes into analyzable components.
- Creating a structured framework to replicate and scale successful strategies.
- Using past achievements as data points to inform future decision-making.

Strategy: Document and analyze the factors that contributed to each success, creating a knowledge base for future problem-solving.

PRINCIPLED PAULA (PERSISTER)

Paula can build on her successes by:

- Aligning achievements with her core values and principles.
- Using victories as proof that ethical approaches can lead to success.
- Leveraging her reputation for integrity to inspire trust in new ventures.

Approach: Frame successes as validation of her principles, using them to reinforce her commitment to ethical practices.

EMPATHETIC EMMA (HARMONIZER)

Emma can capitalize on her victories by:

- Sharing success stories to inspire and motivate others.
- Using achievements to build stronger connections and to foster teamwork.
- Leveraging her successes to create a more supportive work environment.

Tactic: Use past successes as examples of how empathy and collaboration lead to positive outcomes.

CHARISMATIC CHARLIE (PROMOTER)

Charlie can amplify his successes by:

- Turning victories into compelling narratives to inspire others.
- Using past achievements to build credibility for new initiatives.
- Leveraging his charisma to create excitement around future projects.

Method: Frame each success as part of a larger, exciting journey, using it to generate enthusiasm for upcoming challenges.

SPONTANEOUS SAM (REBEL)

Sam can leverage his victories by:

- Using successes as proof that unconventional methods can work.
- Showcasing achievements to challenge traditional approaches.
- Leveraging past wins to gain support for innovative ideas.

Strategy: Present successes as breakthroughs that validate his unique approach to problem-solving.

CONTEMPLATIVE CORY (IMAGINER)

Cory can build on his successes by:

- Using victories as inspiration for new creative projects.
- Leveraging achievements to gain support for his visionary ideas.
- Reflecting on past successes to refine his intuitive decision-making process.

Approach: Use each success as a steppingstone to explore new, more ambitious creative endeavors.

AMBITIOUS AVA (ACHIEVER)

Ava can leverage her victories by:

- Setting increasingly challenging goals based on past achievements.
- Using successes to negotiate for more responsibilities or resources.
- Leveraging her track record to pursue leadership positions.

Tactic: Frame each success as a milestone in a larger career trajectory, using it to justify pursuing more ambitious objectives.

INTUITIVE IAN (DISCERNER)

Ian can capitalize on his successes by:

- Using victories as validation of his intuitive insights.
- Leveraging achievements to gain support for his long-term vision.
- Using past successes to build confidence in his unique perspective.

Method: Present successes as proof of his ability to see patterns and opportunities others might miss.

ADVENTUROUS ANDY (EXPLORER)

Andy can build on his victories by:

- Using successes as launching pads for new, exciting ventures.
- Leveraging achievements to gain support for exploring uncharted territories.
- Using past wins to justify taking calculated risks.

Strategy: Frame each success as an adventure that opens doors to even more thrilling opportunities.

CAUTIOUS CATHY (QUESTIONER)

Cathy can leverage her successes by:

- Thoroughly analyzing victories to identify replicable strategies.
- Using achievements as evidence to support her well-researched proposals.
- Leveraging past successes to build credibility for her meticulous approach.

Approach: Document and present successes with detailed analysis, using them to validate her careful, research-based methods.

DIPLOMATIC DAN (PEACEMAKER)

Dan can capitalize on his victories by:

- Using successes as examples of effective conflict resolution.
- Leveraging achievements to build trust and credibility across diverse groups.
- Using past wins to demonstrate the value of collaborative approaches.

Tactic: Present successes as case studies in effective mediation and team-building.

ORGANIZED OLIVIA (GUARDIAN)

Olivia can build on her successes by:

- Creating detailed records of successful processes for future reference.
- Using achievements to justify implementing more structured systems.
- Leveraging her track record to gain support for her organizational initiatives.

Method: Document each success meticulously, creating templates and best practices for future use.

VISIONARY VICTOR (INNOVATIVE THINKER)

Victor can leverage his victories by:

- Using successes as a proof-of-concept for his innovative ideas.
- Leveraging achievements to gain support for more ambitious, visionary projects.
- Using past wins to inspire and rally teams around new initiatives.

Strategy: Frame each success as steppingstones towards realizing a larger, transformative vision.

SUPPORTIVE SARAH (COUNSELOR)

Sarah can capitalize on her successes by:

- Using victories as examples of effective support and guidance.
- Leveraging achievements to build trust and deepen relationships.
- Using past successes to demonstrate the value of empathetic leadership.

Approach: Present successes as case studies in how supportive environments lead to positive outcomes for individuals and teams.

Here are additional specific, actionable steps for leveraging momentum, along with sections on overcoming setbacks and case studies: Specific, Actionable Steps for Leveraging Momentum:

1. Set Micro-Goals: Break down your larger "possum" into smaller, achievable tasks. Celebrate each micro-goal completion to build momentum.
2. Create a Momentum Tracker: Use a visual tool, like a progress bar or calendar, to track your daily wins. Seeing consistent progress fuels further action.
3. Implement the "Two-Minute Rule": If a task takes less than two minutes, do it immediately. This builds a habit of quick action and prevents small tasks from piling up.
4. Establish a Daily Momentum Routine: Start each day with a small, momentum-building activity related to your goal. This could be as simple as reviewing your goals or doing a quick visualization exercise.

5. Use the "Domino Effect": Identify and focus on the one task that, when completed, will make other tasks easier or unnecessary. This creates a cascade of productivity.
6. Create Accountability Partnerships: Share your daily or weekly goals with an accountability partner. Regular check-ins help maintain momentum.
7. Implement a Reward System: Set up small rewards for consistent action. This could be as simple as a favorite snack after a week of daily progress.

OVERCOMING SETBACKS AND REGAINING LOST MOMENTUM:

1. Acknowledge the Setback: Recognize that setbacks are a normal part of any journey. Don't let them derail your entire progress.
2. Analyze without judgment: Look objectively at what caused the setback. Was it external circumstances, a lack of preparation, or a flaw in your strategy?
3. Adjust Your Approach: Based on your analysis, make necessary adjustments to your plan. This might involve changing your schedule, seeking additional resources, or modifying your goals.
4. Start Small Again: If you've lost significant momentum, don't try to jump back in at full speed. Start with small, easily achievable tasks to rebuild your confidence and momentum.
5. Use Visualization: Spend time visualizing your success and the feeling of regaining your momentum. This can help reignite your motivation.
6. Seek Support: Reach out to your support network. Sometimes an encouraging word or a fresh perspective can help you regain your footing.

7. Practice Self-Compassion: Be kind to yourself. Negative self-talk after a setback can further hinder your progress. Treat yourself as you would a friend facing a similar situation.

CASE STUDIES:

1. Sarah's Weight Loss Journey:
    - Sarah had been trying to lose weight for years. After reading *Eat the Possum*, she decided to leverage momentum in her weight loss journey. She started by setting a micro-goal of walking for ten minutes each day. As she consistently achieved this, she gradually increased the duration and intensity. She used a wall calendar to track her progress, marking each day she exercised with a sticker. This visual representation of her consistency motivated her to keep going. After three months, she had lost fifteen pounds and developed a consistent exercise habit.
2. John's Debt-Free Journey:
    - John was $50,000 in debt and felt overwhelmed. He started by listing all his debts and choosing the smallest one to tackle first (the debt snowball method). He set up automatic payments and used a debt tracker app to visualize his progress. Each time he paid off a debt, he celebrated with a small, budget-friendly reward. This constant sense of progress kept him motivated. When he faced a setback due to an unexpected car repair, he didn't give up. Instead, he adjusted his budget, picked up some extra hours at work, and got back on track. After two and a half years, John became debt-free and now helps others on similar journeys.

3. Emily's Novel Writing Success:
   - Emily had always dreamed of writing a novel but struggled with consistency. She set a micro-goal of writing five hundred words per day. She used a writing app that tracked her daily word count and streaks of consistent writing days. To overcome writer's block, she implemented a two-minute rule: if she felt stuck, she would commit to writing for just two minutes. Often, this small start would lead to a productive writing session. When she missed a day due to illness, she didn't let it derail her. She acknowledged the setback, adjusted her weekly goal, and got back to writing the next day. After eight months of leveraging this momentum, Emily completed her first novel draft.
4. Russell's Revitalized Family Relationship:
   - Russell had been alienated from his daughter for over twenty years. For a long time, he wasn't even sure where she lived. When Russell listened to the *Eat the Possum* message, he was challenged to reestablish his relationship with his daughter. He said it was the hardest thing he had done. He did, and the success encouraged him to grow the relationship. Russell died in a hunting accident about nine months after, and his daughter indicated that she was so thankful that she got to know her daddy again before he died.

CHAPTER 11 QUESTIONS:

1. Reflect on a recent victory in your life. How can you use the momentum from this success to tackle your next challenge or "possum"?

2. The chapter emphasizes the danger of taking a victory lap and losing momentum. Can you identify a time in your life when you lost momentum after a success? How could you have maintained that momentum?
3. How can you apply the author's "next mailbox" philosophy to break down your current challenge into smaller, more manageable steps?
4. This chapter discusses the concept of "proportional potential" in momentum. How can you identify and leverage the energy from your recent successes to fuel your next steps?
5. Considering the story of Elijah, how can you guard against losing momentum when faced with unexpected challenges or threats?
6. The author mentions that momentum works against us if not used immediately. What immediate actions can you take to maintain the momentum from your recent achievements?
7. Review the seven keys to momentum listed in the chapter. Which one resonates most with your current situation, and how can you implement it on your personal change journey this week?

A SUMMARY OF CHAPTER 11 OF *EAT THE POSSUM*:

- Momentum is crucial after a victory; don't stop or become complacent.
- The "great exhale" can be dangerous, leading to loss of progress.
- Momentum has proportional potential and can overcome resistance.
- Use the energy from one victory to fuel the next challenge.

- Seven Keys to Momentum
  - Stop seeing yourself the way others see you.
  - Don't despise small beginnings.
  - Make the most of your current situation.
  - Ignore criticism when your cause is just.
  - Become goal, and reward motivated.
  - Recognize who will fight your battles (God).
  - Create a momentum for victory.
- Additional Insights
  - • Break down large goals into smaller, achievable tasks.
- Use visual tools to track progress.
- Implement daily momentum-building routines.
- Create accountability partnerships.
- Set up reward systems for consistent action.
  - Overcoming Setbacks
    - • Acknowledge setbacks without judgment.
- Analyze causes and adjust strategies.
- Start small when rebuilding momentum.
- Use visualization techniques.
- Seek support and practice self-compassion.
  - Personality-Specific Strategies
    - • The chapter provides tailored approaches for different personality types to leverage momentum.
  - Case Studies
    - • Examples of individuals successfully applying momentum principles in weight loss, debt reduction, and novel writing.
  - Reflection
    - • The chapter encourages readers to reflect on experiences with momentum and apply lessons learned in current situations.
  - Challenges

Remember, the key message is to maintain forward motion after success and use that energy to tackle the next "possum" in your life.

CHAPTER TWELVE
FROM POSSUM TO PLATYPUS: DREAMING BIGGER

When I shared my possum story with the people of our church, they all wanted to know, "Did you eat the possum?" The answer is: Yes! Possum tasted like barbecued pulled pork to me, even though the thought running through my mind said otherwise. That was the only day I have ever eaten or been offered possum barbecue. I can truly say I successfully tasted barbecued opossum. Once you have "tasted" success (see what I did there?), it can set you up for future victories. It must be said that future victories should never stand alone as great gains; instead, they should establish a pattern or culture of victory.

In the sports world, sometimes an underdog wins the contest against a highly favored opponent. Everyone on the winning team celebrates, and it can potentially encourage future game-winning strategies. It also affects the losing team. When highly favored and then losing, it can be so disheartening that it discourages a winning culture, and a defeatist mentality infects the team. The difference is the coach and the perspective that he paints for his team. Depending on the mindset of the team, they can go from being a winning team to losing their season. Winning teams seem to leverage past wins and even losses intentionally to their benefit. They establish and live in a culture of victory.

The other side is just as powerful, for when a losing team suffers a humiliating defeat, it informs how they see themselves.

So, what are the elements to establish a culture of winning, whether eating an opossum or achieving a goal?

Once you have completed the previous steps in this book, the next step is to establish a winning culture. Your victory should not be once-and-done, but one that informs your life and all future battles. You become a winner in life, rather than someone who won a single battle. You have learned that setbacks are not walls, but steppingstones to take you higher than ever.

There will be setbacks. The road to victory is not easy, and setbacks can be disheartening. You almost have to treat your life as you would a football game where you knew your team won before you watched the game.

Several years ago, I recorded my favorite college team football game due to missing it for a wedding I was officiating. After the wedding, I arrived home and immediately received a call from a friend who also loves the same team. He said, "I can't believe we won that game." I stopped him immediately and said, "Don't say another word. I performed a wedding and missed the game. I am going to watch it when we get off of the phone." He apologized, and we finished the call. Based on what he said, I felt assured that we won the game, but I honestly could not see a winning outcome during most of the game. I thought he was referring to another game.

I watched the game, and at the end of the third quarter, we were down three touchdowns. I was certain he was referring to another team, but I continued watching. With about a minute to go in the third quarter, our quarterback threw a pass forty yards and our receiver ran another twenty-five yards and scored a touchdown. The momentum turned, and we owned the fourth quarter, coming back and winning the game.

I was uncertain for a while that we would win, although I was alerted to it by my friend. I could not see it while watching three quarters of the football game. The difference between that team and our season that year was that the coach and players understood how to win. They had a winner's mindset.

First, they had a positive attitude. Even when they were being defeated so soundly, they never gave up. They were hopeful and expectant. Secondly, they were focused and disciplined. They were playing great football, but a few key mistakes had given the opponent the upper hand. They continued to learn. The quarterback was continually studying the other team; even in the midst of the game, he was looking at their defensive scheme and seeking ways to overcome their opposition. He recognized the value of his teammates and continued to express confidence in them and appreciation for their hard work. He also took responsibility for his own mistakes. One errant pass was intercepted and returned for a touchdown. Another time, he fumbled, and the opponent recovered, and eventually that mistake ended in another touchdown. The quarterback and coach were used to comebacks and were confident they could learn, adapt, and overcome the challenges. Watching the first three quarters, I was not as confident. I, however, did not matter.

Neither do the people who don't believe you can win.

They don't matter, and once you have a history of winning, despite what others believe, you can experience even greater victories because you know you, you know God, and you have experience in winning when others would give up.

This was a sports analogy, but it is valid when presented with hard things. Do not trust what you are seeing! It may mean defeat, but the greatest victories are always discounted when someone is backed against the wall.

Here are some relatable things about my story. First, maintain fundamentals regardless, instead of relying on finesse. For the person desiring to lose weight, healthy eating and exercise can benefit their weight loss goal. Communication and intimacy are vital fundamentals to increase marital satisfaction for the one whose marriage is struggling. For the one struggling with addiction, separating yourself from the addictive item and people who use it is fundamental to increasing the likelihood of success. Of all the things, the fundamentals are not always enough to gain victory, but they are vital to success.

Second, adjust when necessary. If something is not working, it is not a call to quit. It is a challenge to adapt. Not every strategy works; ask any dietician. Diets sometimes need to be tailored to the lifestyle and the metabolism of the individual, diseases or chronic conditions they may possess, and a host of other considerations. One thing may work for one person, but it may not work for you, and if it doesn't, adjust! Frankly, that is why we included so much information related to personality types in *Eat the Possum*.

Third, look at every obstacle as an opportunity. This perspective key is vital to success. Once my daughter was doing math homework on the way home from school. She was frustrated because the math concepts were a challenge to her. I looked at her and said, "What are you doing?"

"Math problems," she replied with a sigh of despair.

"They are not math problems," I offered.

"Yes, they are math problems," she said.

"They are not math problems, nope... not math problems."

"Daddy, it says it right here, MATH PROBLEMS," she noted as she pointed to the words 'Math Problems' in the header.

"They are not math problems," I replied matter-of-factly.

"If they are not math problems, what are they?" she asked.

"They are math opportunities."

She laughed and laughed, maybe cried a little, and then threw the book at me. She has never forgotten that "math lesson." Thankfully, she started speaking to me again a short time later.

BIBLICALLY BASED GUIDED VISUALIZATION EXERCISES:

1. The Promised Land Visualization:
    - Close your eyes and imagine yourself standing where Moses stood, overlooking the Promised Land (Deuteronomy 34:1-4). Visualize the lush valleys, flowing rivers, and abundant resources. Now, picture your own "Promised Land"—the fulfillment of your goals and dreams. What does it look like? How does it feel to be there?
2. David's Victory Visualization:
    - Picture yourself as David, facing your own Goliath (1 Samuel 17). Feel the smooth stones in your hand, the confidence in your heart. Visualize yourself defeating your challenge with God's strength. See yourself victorious, just as David was.
3. Joseph's Dream Fulfillment:
    - Imagine yourself as Joseph, seeing your dreams come to fruition after years of hardship (Genesis 37-50). Visualize the journey from the pit to the palace. Picture yourself overcoming obstacles and ultimately achieving your God-given vision.

SETTING SMART GOALS ALIGNED WITH BIG DREAMS:

1. Specific: Clearly define your goal. Instead of "I want to serve God better," try, "I will volunteer at the local food bank every Saturday morning."
2. Measurable: Quantify your goal. For example, "I will read through the entire Bible in one year by reading three chapters daily."
3. Achievable: Ensure your goal is realistic. "I will increase my tithing by 1 percent each month until I

reach 10 percent," is more achievable than, "I will give away all my possessions immediately."
4. Relevant: Align your goal with your values and bigger dreams. If your dream is to become a missionary, a relevant goal might be, "I will enroll in a cross-cultural communication course this semester."
5. Time-bound: Set a deadline. "I will start a weekly prayer group in my neighborhood within the next two months," gives you a clear timeframe.

SCIENTIFIC RESEARCH ON POSITIVE THINKING AND VISUALIZATION:

1. A study published in the *Journal of Personality and Social Psychology* found that positive visualization can increase motivation and goal attainment.[1]
2. Research showed that mental imagery activates similar brain regions as actual performance, suggesting visualization can improve skills.[2]
3. A study in the *Journal of Consulting and Clinical Psychology* demonstrated that positive thinking interventions can significantly reduce symptoms of depression and anxiety.[3]

---

1. Gabriele Oettingen and Doris Mayer, "The Motivating Function of Thinking About the Future: Expectations Versus Fantasies," Journal of Personality and Social Psychology 83, no. 5 (2002): 1198-1212.
2. K. M. O'Craven and N. Kanwisher, "Mental Imagery of Faces and Places Activates Corresponding Stimulus-Specific Brain Regions," Journal of Cognitive Neuroscience 12, no. 6 (2000): 1013-23, https://doi.org/10.1162/08989290051137549.
3. Linda Bolier, Merel Haverman, Gerben J. Westerhof, Heleen Riper, Filip Smit, and Ernst Bohlmeijer, "Positive Psychology Interventions: A Meta-Analysis of Randomized Controlled Studies," BMC Public Health 13, no. 1 (2013): 119.

BIBLICAL CHARACTERS WHO USED VISUALIZATION:

1. Abraham: God told him to look at the stars to visualize his numerous descendants (Genesis 15:5).
2. Joshua: God instructed him to visualize victory before the battle of Jericho (Joshua 6:2-5).
3. Ezekiel: He used vivid mental imagery in his prophecies, such as the valley of dry bones (Ezekiel 37:1-14).
4. Paul: He encouraged believers to set their minds on things above, essentially visualizing their heavenly citizenship (Colossians 3:1-2).

Our mindset regarding the problem may be as much of the problem as the problem itself. If so, we have to change the way we think about it. If we fail to change the way we think about it, we will lose the battle. It affects our morale and motivation, creates inner conflict, and weakens us in other areas.

The opposite is true as well. If we have a positive mindset, it will breed further victories. Those victories may not become world-wide successes, but they do provide us the ability to leverage them for future endeavors.

Let's face it: eating barbecued possum may not be the very thing that changes our lives. It may not be the hardest thing we have ever endeavored, nor the most distasteful thing we have eaten, but besides being fodder for a book, it does allow us to experience what Cletus said: "If you learn how to do it, you will eat some great barbecue, and you may also win at life. But if you shy away from this small challenge, the next hard thing may become overwhelming."

I am glad I ate it, and I am glad it provided me with the courage to face the most distasteful things in my life. So go ahead and eat the possum and win!

CHAPTER 12 QUESTIONS:

1. Reflecting on your recent "possum eating" experience, how can you use this victory to establish a pattern or culture of success in other areas of your life?
2. The chapter emphasizes the importance of maintaining a winning mindset. How can the "next mailbox" philosophy help you break down large goals into smaller, manageable steps?
3. Consider a recent setback in your life. How can you reframe it as a learning opportunity or a steppingstone towards eventual success, as described in the football game analogy?
4. The author discusses the importance of maintaining fundamentals. What are the core "fundamentals" in your current challenge, and how can you ensure you're consistently practicing them?
5. How can you apply the concept of "math opportunities" instead of "math problems" to the challenges you're currently facing in your personal change journey?
6. The chapter introduces biblically based guided visualization exercises. Which of these resonates most with you, and how can you incorporate it into your daily routine to reinforce your goals?
7. Considering the SMART goal-setting framework presented, how can you refine one of your current goals to make it more Specific, Measurable, Achievable, Relevant, and Time-bound?

A SUMMARY OF CHAPTER 12 OF *EAT YOUR POSSUM*:

- Success breeds success: Tasting victory, even in small

challenges like eating possum, can set you up for future wins.
- Establish a culture of victory: Don't let wins be isolated events; use them to create a pattern of success in your life.
- Mindset matters: A winning mentality can turn setbacks into steppingstones for greater achievements.
- Maintain fundamentals: Stick to core practices that contribute to your goal, even when facing challenges.
- Be adaptable: If a strategy isn't working, be willing to adjust rather than give up.
- Reframe obstacles as opportunities: Change your perspective on challenges to see them as chances for growth.
- Use visualization: Employ biblically based guided visualization exercises to reinforce your goals and dreams.
- Set SMART goals: Make your objectives Specific, Measurable, Achievable, Relevant, and Time-bound.
- Learn from setbacks: Use failures as learning experiences to inform future strategies.
- Stay positive: Maintain a hopeful and expectant attitude, even when facing difficulties.
- Take responsibility: Own your mistakes and use them as opportunities for improvement.
- Focus on what you can control: Don't let others' doubts affect your belief in your ability to succeed.
- Leverage past wins: Use previous successes, no matter how small, to build confidence for future challenges.

Remember: the journey to success is not always easy, but maintaining a winning mindset and learning from each experience can help you overcome obstacles and achieve your goals.

· · ·

In this section, I have included a detailed list of notes, references, research and citations for each book chapter. There is a vast amount of scientific literature and Biblical wisdom that aligns with the principles presented in "EAT THE POSSUM." While the premise may seem whimsical, we believe these principles are grounded in solid research and timeless truths that can empower readers to tackle their toughest challenges.

The scientific studies cited here provide empirical support for the book's key ideas about resilience, adaptability, and overcoming adversity. Of course, scientific understanding evolves over time, so some details may require future updates. However, the foundational Scriptural principles remain constant, offering enduring guidance. This compilation of notes aims to enhance the reader's appreciation of the evidence underpinning each chapter. It demonstrates how playful metaphors about possums connect to serious insights from both science and Scripture. We hope these references will deepen your understanding and inspire further exploration of these empowering concepts. If you notice any errors or have questions about the citations, please don't hesitate to contact the author at johnutley@cottonhouse.press. We strive for accuracy and welcome reader feedback to improve this resource continually.

POSSUM NOTES
THE JUICY BITS BEHIND THE BARBECUE

In this section, I have included a detailed list of notes, references, research and citations for each book chapter. There is a vast amount of scientific literature and Biblical wisdom that aligns with the principles presented in "EAT THE POSSUM." While the premise may seem whimsical, we believe these principles are grounded in solid research and timeless truths that can empower readers to tackle their toughest challenges.

The scientific studies cited here provide empirical support for the book's key ideas about resilience, adaptability, and overcoming adversity. Of course, scientific understanding evolves over time, so some details may require future updates. However, the foundational Scriptural principles remain constant, offering enduring guidance. This compilation of notes aims to enhance the reader's appreciation of the evidence underpinning each chapter. It demonstrates how playful metaphors about possums connect to serious insights from both science and Scripture. We hope these references will deepen your understanding and inspire further exploration of these empowering concepts. If you notice any errors or have questions about the citations, please don't hesitate to contact the author at johnutley@cottonhouse.

press. We strive for accuracy and welcome reader feedback to improve this resource continually.

CHAPTER 1

1. Growth Mindset and Resilience:
    - Dweck's research on growth mindset aligns with the chapter's emphasis on overcoming challenges. Studies show that individuals with a growth mindset are more resilient and persistent in facing difficulties.
    - Dweck, C. S. (2006). Mindset: The New Psychology of Success. Random House Publishing Group.

2. Positive Adaptation to Challenges:
    - Seery et al.'s research supports the idea that overcoming challenges can lead to personal growth and increased resilience.
    - Seery, M. D., Holman, E. A., & Silver, R. C. (2010). Whatever does not kill us: Cumulative lifetime adversity, vulnerability, and resilience. Journal of Personality and Social Psychology, 99(6), 1025–1041.

3. Social Support in Overcoming Challenges:
    - Cohen and Wills' study emphasizes the importance of social support in handling adversity, which aligns with the chapter's discussion on the role of relationships in overcoming obstacles.
    - Cohen, S., & Wills, T. A. (1985). Stress, social support, and the buffering hypothesis. Psychological Bulletin, 98(2), 310.

4. Coping Strategies:
   - Lazarus and Folkman's research on coping strategies corresponds with the chapter's focus on developing effective ways to handle challenges.
   - Lazarus, R. S., & Folkman, S. (1984). Stress, appraisal, and coping. Springer Publishing Company.

5. Resilience Resources:
   - Fullerton et al.'s study on resilience resources and their interaction with coping responses supports the chapter's discussion on leveraging personal strengths to overcome challenges.
   - Fullerton DJ, Zhang LM, Kleitman S (2021) An integrative process model of resilience in an academic context: Resilience resources, coping strategies, and positive adaptation. PLoS ONE 16(2): e0246000.

6. Character Strengths and Resilience:
   - Martínez-Martí and Ruch's research on the relationship between character strengths and resilience aligns with the chapter's emphasis on leveraging personal traits to overcome obstacles.
   - Martínez-Martí, M. L., & Ruch, W. (2017). Character strengths predict resilience over and above positive affect, self-efficacy, optimism, social support, self-esteem, and life satisfaction. The Journal of Positive Psychology, 12(2), 110–119.

7. Developmental Cascades in Resilience:
   - Masten and Tellegen's work on developmental cascades in resilience supports the chapter's discussion on how overcoming one challenge can lead to growth in other areas.

- Masten, A. S., & Tellegen, A. (2012). Resilience in developmental psychopathology: Contributions of the project competence longitudinal study. Development and Psychopathology, 24(2), 345-361.

8. Five-Factor Model:
   - This study provides evidence for the universality of the Five-Factor Model of personality across cultures.
   - McCrae, R. R., & Costa, P. T. (1997). Personality trait structure as a human universal. American Psychologist, 52(5), 509–516.

9. Personality and Leadership:
   - This meta-analysis by Judge, et.al (2002) examines the relationship between personality traits and leadership effectiveness.
   - Judge, T. A., Bono, J. E., Ilies, R., & Gerhardt, M. W. (2002). Personality and leadership: A qualitative and quantitative review. Journal of Applied Psychology, 87(4), 765–780.

10. Personality and Job Performance:
    - This influential meta-analysis explores how the Big Five personality traits relate to job performance across various occupations.
    - Barrick, M. R., & Mount, M. K. (1991). The Big Five personality dimensions and job performance: A meta-analysis. Personnel Psychology, 44(1), 1–26.

11. Personality and Performance:
    - This study examines how personality traits relate specifically to sales performance. While this research compares personality type with employee

performance, it also provides a template for performance metrics in other goal related ideals.
- Furnham, A., & Fudge, C. (2008). The Five Factor model of personality and sales performance. Journal of Individual Differences, 29(1), 11–16.

12. Five-Factor Personality Model: This review article provides a comprehensive overview of the development and evidence of the Five-Factor Model of personality.
    - Digman, J. M. (1990). Personality structure: Emergence of the five-factor model. Annual Review of Psychology, 41(1), 417-440.

13. Structure of Personality Traits: This seminal paper discusses the structure and universality of personality traits.
    - Goldberg, L. R. (1993). The structure of phenotypic personality traits. American Psychologist, 48(1), 26–34.

CHAPTER 2

1. Neurobiological Basis of Courage:
    - This study explores the neural mechanisms underlying courageous behavior, aligning with the chapter's discussion of the biological aspects of courage.
    - Nili, Uri, Gabriel Goldberg, Aya Weizman, and Yadin Dudai. "Fear Thou Not: Activity of Frontal and Temporal Circuits in Moments of Real-Life Courage." Neuron 66, no. 6 (2010): 949-962.

2. Courage and Resilience:
    - This research supports the chapter's emphasis on the relationship between courage and resilience in facing life's challenges.
    - Koerner, Melissa M. "Courage as Identity Work: Accounts of Workplace Courage." Academy of Management Journal 57, no. 1 (2014): 63-93.

3. Moral Courage in Leadership:
    - This study aligns with the chapter's discussion on moral courage and its importance in leadership roles.
    - Hannah, Sean T., Bruce J. Avolio, and Fred O. Walumbwa. "Relationships between Authentic Leadership, Moral Courage, and Ethical and Pro-Social Behaviors." Business Ethics Quarterly 21, no. 4 (2011): 555-578.

4. Courage and Personal Growth:
    - This research supports the chapter's assertion that courageous actions lead to personal growth and development.
    - Pury, Cynthia L. S., and Shane J. Lopez. "Courage." In The Oxford Handbook of Positive Psychology, edited by Shane J. Lopez and C. R. Snyder, 375-382. New York: Oxford University Press, 2009.

5. Courage in Daily Life:
    - This study examines everyday acts of courage, supporting the chapter's discussion on small, daily courageous actions.
    - Woodard, Cooper R., and Cynthia L. S. Pury. "The Construct of Courage: Categorization and

Measurement." Consulting Psychology Journal: Practice and Research 59, no. 2 (2007): 135-147.

6. Courage and Fear Management:
   - This research aligns with the chapter's exploration of courage as a means of managing and overcoming fear.
   - Norton, Peter J., and Brandon A. Weiss. "The Role of Courage on Behavioral Approach in a Fear-Eliciting Situation: A Proof-of-Concept Pilot Study." Journal of Anxiety Disorders 23, no. 2 (2009): 212-217.

7. Courage and Self-Efficacy:
   - This study supports the chapter's discussion on the relationship between courage and self-confidence.
   - Muris, Peter. "A Brief Questionnaire for Measuring Self-Efficacy in Youths." Journal of Psychopathology and Behavioral Assessment 23, no. 3 (2001): 145-149.

8. Courage in Adolescence:
   - This research aligns with the chapter's emphasis on developing courage during formative years.
   - Bronk, Kendall Cotton, and Brian R. Riches. "The Role of Purpose and Moral Development in the Development of Courage in Adolescence." Human Development 60, no. 6 (2017): 279-341.

CHAPTER 3

On the effectiveness of the "Five Whys" technique: This research discusses the benefits of the Five Why's technique in problem-solving and continuous improvement, aligning with the book's emphasis on identifying root causes.

1. Serrat, O. (2017). The Five Whys Technique. In Knowledge Solutions (pp. 307-310). Springer, Singapore.

2. Easy Problem Solving:
    - Haury provides a simple process for root cause analysis.
    - Haury, Jennifer. "Easy Problem Solving Using the 4-step Method." https://mrsc.org/stay-informed/mrsc-insight/june-2017/4-step-problem-solving-method

3. Regarding root cause analysis in healthcare:
    - This study examines the effectiveness and limitations of root cause analysis in healthcare settings, which relates to the book's discussion on identifying underlying issues.
    - Peerally, M. F., Carr, S., Waring, J., & Dixon-Woods, M. (2017). The problem with root cause analysis. BMJ Quality & Safety, 26(5), 417-422.

4. On the importance of identifying root causes in problem-solving:
    - This work provides a comprehensive overview of root cause analysis techniques, supporting the book's emphasis on thoroughly understanding problems before attempting solutions.

- Andersen, B., & Fagerhaug, T. (2006). Root cause analysis: simplified tools and techniques. ASQ Quality Press.

5. Regarding the role of emotions in forgiveness and problem-solving:
    - This research explores the emotional aspects of forgiveness, which aligns with the book's discussion on reconciliation and addressing root causes of conflicts.
    - Worthington Jr, E. L., & Scherer, M. (2004). Forgiveness is an emotion-focused coping strategy that can reduce health risks and promote health resilience: Theory, review, and hypotheses. Psychology & Health, 19(3), 385-405.

On the importance of systems thinking in problem-solving:

This work emphasizes the importance of systems thinking in addressing complex problems, supporting the book's approach to looking beyond surface-level issues.

Leveson, N. (2011). Engineering a safer world: Systems thinking applied to safety. MIT press.

ADDITIONAL REFERENCE MATERIAL

Montesi, L., M. El Ghoch, L. Brodosi, S. Calugi, G. Marchesini, and R. Dalle Grave. "Long-term Weight Loss Maintenance for Obesity: A Multidisciplinary Approach." Diabetes, Metabolic Syndrome and Obesity: Targets and Therapy 9 (2016): 37-46.

Centers for Medicare & Medicaid Services. "Five Whys Tool for Root Cause Analysis." Accessed October 15, 2024. https://www.cms.gov/medicare/provider-enrollment-and-certification/qapi/downloads/fivewhys.pdf.

BusinessMap. "Unlock the Power of 5 Whys: Root Cause Analysis Made Easy." Accessed October 15, 2024. https://businessmap.io/lean-management/improvement/5-whys-analysis-tool.

MaxGrip. "The Five Why Analysis – A Simple Yet Effective RCA Tool." Accessed October 15, 2024. https://www.maxgrip.com/resource/the-five-why-analysis-a-simple-yet-effective-rca-tool/.

Reliability. "Root Cause Analysis with 5 Whys Technique (With Examples)." Accessed October 15, 2024. https://reliability.com/resources/articles/5-whys-root-cause-analysis/.

Lucidchart. "How to Conduct a 5 Whys Analysis." Accessed October 15, 2024. https://www.lucidchart.com/blog/5-whys-analysis.

Rupa Health. "5 Conditions That Make It Harder To Lose Weight." Accessed October 15, 2024. https://www.rupahealth.com/post/cant-lose-weight-these-5-medical-problems-may-be-why.

Tulip. "What Are the Five Whys? A Tool For Root Cause Analysis." Accessed October 15, 2024. https://tulip.co/glossary/five-whys/.

Gunnars, Kris. "14 Common Reasons You're Not Losing Weight." Healthline, August 30, 2023. https://www.healthline.com/nutrition/20-reasons-you-are-not-losing-weight.

CHAPTER 4

1. The importance of positive peer relationships for academic achievement and well-being:
    - Shao investigates the complex interplay between social support, basic psychological needs satisfaction and the potential for success positive peer relationships provide.
    - Shao, Y., Kang, S., Lu, Q. *et al.* How peer relationships affect academic achievement among junior high school students: The chain mediating roles of learning motivation and learning engagement. *BMC Psychol* **12**, 278 (2024). https://doi.org/10.1186/s40359-024-01780-z https://bmcpsychology.biomedcentral.com/articles/10.1186/s40359-024-01780-z

2. The potential negative effects of peer influence:
    - This study provides warning concerning the effect toxic relationships and social circles have on adolescents.
    - Karakos H. Positive Peer Support or Negative Peer Influence? The Role of Peers among Adolescents in Recovery High Schools. Peabody J Educ. 2014 Jan 1; 89(2):214-228. doi: 10.1080/0161956X.2014.897094. PMID: 24839335; PMCID: PMC4019403.

3. The positive relationship between spirituality and well-being:
    - This study highlights the relationship between spiritually and health-related behaviors are positively related to psychological well-being.

- Bożek A, Nowak PF, Blukacz M. The Relationship Between Spirituality, Health-Related Behavior, and Psychological Well-Being. Front Psychol. 2020 Aug 14; 11:1997. doi: 10.3389/fpsyg.2020.01997. PMID: 32922340; PMCID: PMC7457021.

4. The importance of social connectedness for mental and physical health:
    - This study by Galloway and Hoppe examines the impact of social connectedness and spirituality on depression and perceived health among rural residents. The researchers found a significant positive correlation between social connectedness and overall well-being. Specifically, individuals who reported feeling more socially connected tended to perceive themselves as having better physical and mental health. Moreover, higher levels of social connectedness were associated with fewer reported depressive symptoms.
    - Galloway, Ann P., Melissa Henry. "Relationships between Social Connectedness and Spirituality and Depression and Perceived Health Status of Rural Residents." Online Journal of Rural Nursing and Healthcare, Vol 14, No. 2 (2014).
    - https://rnojournal.binghamton.edu/index.php/RNO/article/view/325

5. The adaptive function of peer influence in adolescence:
    - This comprehensive review by Laursen and Veenstra examines the critical role of peer influence during adolescence. The authors argue that adolescents' heightened susceptibility to peer influence is not a weakness, but rather an adaptive

response to the significant structural changes occurring during this developmental period.
- Laursen B, Veenstra R. Toward understanding the functions of peer influence: A summary and synthesis of recent empirical research. J Res Adolesc. 2021 Dec; 31(4):889-907. doi: 10.1111/jora.12606. PMID: 34820944; PMCID: PMC8630732.
- While this research focuses on adolescents, it supports the general principle in the chapter about the significant impact of one's social circle on personal development and decision-making.

ADDITIONAL REFERENCE MATERIAL

Elephant Learning. "Michael Jordan: Cut From High School Team, Became an NBA Superstar." Accessed May 15, 2024. https://www.elephantlearning.com/post/michael-jordan-cut-from-high-school-team-became-nba-superstar.

Lofton Jr., Lloyd. "12 Tips for Building a Support Network." LinkedIn, Accessed October 15, 2024. https://www.linkedin.com/pulse/12-tips-building-support-network-lloyd-lofton-jr-l-u-t-c-.

TechTrone. "How to Build a Support Network." Accessed October 15, 2024. https://www.techtrone.com/how-to-build-a-support-network/.

Warrior Mindset. "Chapter 11: Developing a Support System." Accessed June 1, 2024. https://warriormindset.us/chapter-11-developing-a-support-system/.

CHAPTER 5

1. Research found that procrastination is associated with subsequent mental health problems, unhealthy lifestyle behaviors, and worse psychosocial health factors. This aligns with the chapter's emphasis on the importance of urgency and avoiding procrastination. A study by Ziegler et al. (2024) demonstrated that procrastination leads to depression and anxiety symptoms over time, highlighting the negative consequences of delaying action.
    - Johansson F, Rozental A, Edlund K, Côté P, Sundberg T, Onell C, Rudman A, Skillgate E. Associations Between Procrastination and Subsequent Health Outcomes Among University Students in Sweden. JAMA Netw Open. 2023 Jan 3; 6(1): e2249346. doi: 10.1001/jamanetworkopen.2022.49346. PMID: 36598789; PMCID: PMC9857662.
    - Ziegler, Matthias, Tabea Scheel, Carolin Goetz, and Markus Bühner. "Procrastination, Depression and Anxiety Symptoms in University Students: A Longitudinal Study." BMC Psychology 12, no. 1 (2024): 97. https://doi.org/10.1186/s40359-024-01542-x.

The 5-Second Rule

2. While there are no specific studies on Mel Robbins' 5-Second Rule, research on cognitive and behavioral psychology supports the concept of quick action in overcoming procrastination. The rule's emphasis on immediate action aligns with strategies for tackling procrastination and encouraging productivity.

- Jochmann, A., Gusy, B., Lesener, T. *et al.* Procrastination, depression and anxiety symptoms in university students: a three-wave longitudinal study on the mediating role of perceived stress. *BMC Psychol* **12**, 276 (2024). https://doi.org/10.1186/s40359-024-01761-2

The Pomodoro Technique

3. A personal exploration study by a UCLA student found that implementing the Pomodoro Technique resulted in a 46% decrease in distractions and increased motivation and focus during study sessions. This supports the chapter's recommendation of using techniques to create urgency and focus.
   - Anonymous. "The Effect of Focus Sessions and Periodic Breaks on Studying: A Personal Exploration of the Pomodoro Technique." Writineering, UCLA, June 16, 2020. https://writineering.humspace.ucla.edu/student-work/the-effect-of-focus-sessions-and-periodic-breaks-on-studying-a-personal-exploration-of-the-pomodoro-technique/. https://www.counselling-directory.org.uk/memberarticles/what-are-the-effects-of-procrastination-on-mental-health

Urgency of Decision-Making

4. Research on the importance of urgency in decision-making based on dynamic information suggests that decisions are better explained by an urgency-gating mechanism than by an accumulation process in certain situations. This aligns with the chapter's emphasis on quick decision-making and action.

- Ferrucci, Lorenzo, Aldo Genovesio, and Encarni Marcos. "The Importance of Urgency in Decision Making Based on Dynamic Information." PLOS Computational Biology 17, no. 10 (2021): e1009455. https://doi.org/10.1371/journal.pcbi.1009455. https://proactivitylab.com/decoding-mel-robbins-5-second-rule/#google_vignette

The Illusion of Urgency

5. A study published in the PMC (2023) discusses the concept of the "illusion of urgency" and the importance of distinguishing between truly urgent tasks and those that only appear urgent. This relates to the chapter's focus on creating genuine urgency for important tasks.
    - Puckett, Yvette, Kimberly A. Boynton, and Alison L. Chetlen. "The Illusion of Urgency." Journal of the American College of Radiology 20, no. 5 (2023): 629-631. https://doi.org/10.1016/j.jacr.2023.01.025.

6. The effect of Pomodoro technique on student Mendelian genetics concept mastery during synchronous remote learning.
    - International Research Journal of Management, IT and Social Sciences,
    - 10(4), 233–243. https://doi.org/10.21744/irjmis.v10n4.2287

ADDITIONAL REFERENCE MATERIAL

https://pmc.ncbi.nlm.nih.gov/articles/PMC10159458/

University of Georgia Extension. "Time Management: 10 Strategies for Better Time Management." Accessed October 15, 2024. https://extension.uga.edu/publications/detail.html?number=C1042&title=time-management-10-strategies-for-better-time-management.

Reddit. "Any Tips for Better Time Management?" r/TimeManagement. Accessed October 15, 2024. https://www.reddit.com/r/TimeManagement/comments/12lpaah/any_tips_for_better_time_management/.

Upwork. "Time Management Strategies." Accessed October 15, 2024. https://www.upwork.com/resources/time-management-strategies.

Strategic People Solutions. "Effective Time Management: Avoiding the Tyranny of the Urgent." Accessed October 15, 2024. https://strategicpeoplesolutions.com/posts/effective-time-management-avoiding-tyranny-urgent/.

Entrepreneur. "15 Time Management Tips for Achieving Your Goals." Accessed October 15, 2024. https://www.entrepreneur.com/living/15-time-management-tips-for-achieving-your-goals/299336.

CHAPTER 6

1. Visualization and Mental Imagery:
   - Research has shown that visualization techniques can enhance motivation, boost confidence, and improve problem-solving skills. A study by Morin & Latham (2000) found that visualization exercises increased focus and enhanced goal setting in business settings.
   - Holloway, Jeremy C. "Visualization for Growth Mindset of Underrepresented College Students." PhD diss., The University of Toledo, 2020. https://etd.ohiolink.edu/acprod/odb_etd/ws/send_file/send?accession=toledo1588599835366586&disposition=inline.

2. Mindset Shifts:
   - Studies have demonstrated that visualization exercises can positively impact students' academic motivation and resilience. A dissertation by Grace Tyson found that visualization techniques helped change student mindsets and increase their confidence in overcoming challenges.
   - Tyson, Grace. "Visualization for Growth Mindset of Underrepresented College Students." PhD diss., University of Toledo, 2020. https://etd.ohiolink.edu/acprod/odb_etd/ws/send_file/send?accession=toledo1588599835366586&disposition=inline.

3. Parable-based Teaching:
   - Jesus's use of parables as a teaching method has been studied extensively. Dillon (2005) suggests that parables made up 27% of Jesus' teaching time

and were used to deliver complex messages in an accessible format.
   - Dillon, James T. Jesus as a Teacher: A Multidisciplinary Case Study. Eugene, OR: Wipf & Stock, 2005.

4. Fønnebø explores the use of visually encouraged parables enabling illumination of the principles to further encourage personal transformation.
   - Fønnebø, Liv. "The Parables: The Transforming Leadership Tools of the Master." Journal of Applied Christian Leadership 5, no. 1 (Spring 2011): 20-28.

5. Cognitive Learning Theory:
   - The concept of "high road transfer" in cognitive learning theory aligns with Jesus's use of parables. This process involves formulating new abstractions or "rules" in a person's life through profound understanding (Biehler & Snowman, 1993).
   - Biehler, Robert F., and Jack Snowman. Psychology Applied to Teaching. 7th ed. Boston: Houghton Mifflin, 1993.

6. Neuroscience of Storytelling:
   - Bergen (2012) explains that when we hear language about actions or objects, we use the same brain pathways to visualize it as if we were actually performing the action. This supports the effectiveness of parables and visualization techniques in learning.
   - Bergen, Benjamin K. Louder Than Words: The New Science of How the Mind Makes Meaning. New York: Basic Books, 2012.

7. Olson examines Jesus' use of parables as an effective oral training method for making disciples, teaching people, bridging cultures, and transforming lives. Olson explores how parables serve as both mirrors and windows, reflecting human nature while revealing divine truths.
   - Olson, Kevin. "Jesus and the Parables: A Compelling Oral Training Tool." First Fruits Papers, Asbury Theological Seminary, accessed October 18, 2024. https://place.asburyseminary.edu/cgi/viewcontent.cgi?article=1034&context=firstfruitspapers.

8. Learning Styles and Parabolic Method:
   - Foster and Moran (1985) draw parallels between Piaget's learning theory and Jesus' parabolic method, suggesting that both involve activating the learner's existing knowledge, creating cognitive disequilibrium, and providing guidance to reach a higher level of understanding.
   - Foster, James D., and Glenn T. Moran. "Piaget and Parables: The Convergence of Secular and Scriptural Views of Learning." Journal of Psychology and Theology 13, no. 2 (1985): 97-103. https://digitalcommons.georgefox.edu/cgi/viewcontent.cgi?params=%2Fcontext%2Fgscp_fac%2Farticle%2F1074%2F&path_info=Foster_1985_13_2.pdf.

9. Effectiveness of Parables:
   - Kistemaker's research highlights that parables often teach their basic truth through the use of contrast or a single comparison within the story, making them effective in conveying complex ideas.

- Kistemaker, Simon J. The Parables: Understanding the Stories Jesus Told. Grand Rapids: Baker Books, 2002.
- Barnes, Terry. "Matthew's Parable of the Talents: A Story of Faith." Master's thesis, Calvary Theological Seminary, 2006. https://digitalcommons.liberty.edu/cgi/viewcontent.cgi?article=1113&context=fac_dis.

ADDITIONAL REFERENCE MATERIAL

Pham, Lien B., and Shelley E. Taylor. "From Thought to Action: Effects of Process-Versus Outcome-Based Mental Simulations on Performance." Personality and Social Psychology Bulletin 25, no. 2 (1999): 250-260.

Beck, Aaron T. "Cognitive Therapy: Nature and Relation to Behavior Therapy." Behavior Therapy 1, no. 2 (1970): 184-200.

Oettingen, Gabriele, Heather Barry Kappes, Katie B. Guttenberg, and Peter M. Gollwitzer. "Self-regulation of Time Management: Mental Contrasting with Implementation Intentions." European Journal of Social Psychology 45, no. 2 (2015): 218-229.

Riding, Richard, and Indra Cheema. "Cognitive Styles—An Overview and Integration." Educational Psychology 11, no. 3-4 (1991): 193-215.

White, Michael, and David Epston. Narrative Means to Therapeutic Ends. New York: W. W. Norton & Company, 1990.

CHAPTER 7

1. On the importance of resilience and its relationship to personality traits:
   - "Resilience refers to the process by which individuals use the ability to cope with challenges to successfully adapt to adverse situations, maintaining or recovering their physical and psychological health,"
   - Rodríguez-Fernández, A., Ramos-Díaz, E., Axpe-Saez, I., & Ferrándiz-Vindel, I. M. (2022). Relation between resilience and personality traits: The role of hopelessness and age. PloS one, 17(9), e0274620.

2. On perfectionism as a potential hidden challenge:
   - "Perfectionism derives from anxiety or self-esteem issues, which themselves have been linked to less personal satisfaction and an increased risk of suicide,"
   - Kearns, H., Forbes, A., & Gardiner, M. (2007). Your Best Life: Perfectionism—The Bane of Happiness. Clinical Orthopaedics and Related Research, 467(1), 2079-2083.

3. On building resilience through multiple factors:
   - "Determinants of resilience include personality traits, genetic/epigenetic modifications of genes involved in the stress response, cognitive and behavioral flexibility, secure attachment with a caregiver, social and community support systems, nutrition and exercise, and alignment of circadian rhythm to the natural light/dark cycle,"
   - Agorastos, A., & Olff, M. (2023). Resilience by design: How nature, nurture, environment, and

epigenetics shape stress response. European Journal of Psychotraumatology, 14(1), 2206282.

4. On the relationship between academic self-efficacy and resilience:
   - "ASE was correlated with, and a significant predictor of, academic resilience and students exhibited greater academic resilience when responding to vicarious adversity compared to personal adversity,"
   - Cassidy, S. (2015). Resilience Building in Students: The Role of Academic Self-Efficacy. Frontiers in Psychology, 6, 1781.

5. This study investigates the complex relationships between gratitude, personality traits, career resilience, and career success among Chinese college students. Using a sample of 444 students, the researchers employ structural equation modeling to examine how gratitude influences career success through the mediating role of career resilience.
   - Xu, Jian, and Yuanping Jiang. "The Influence of Gratitude and Personality Traits on Career Resilience and Career Success Among College Students." Frontiers in Psychology 15 (2024): 1340200. https://doi.org/10.3389/fpsyg.2024.1340200.

ADDITIONAL RESEARCH MATERIAL

Cross, R., Dillon, K., & Greenberg, D. (2021). The Secret to Building Resilience. Harvard Business Review.

ADDITIONAL REFERENCE MATERIAL

Bleidorn, Wiebke, Christopher J. Hopwood, and Richard E. Lucas. "Life Events and Personality Trait Change." Journal of Personality 86, no. 1 (2018): 83-96.

Oshio, Atsushi, Kanako Taku, Mari Hirano, and Gul Saeed. "Resilience and Big Five Personality Traits: A Meta-Analysis." Personality and Individual Differences 127 (2018): 54-60.

Bonanno, George A., and Erica D. Diminich. "Annual Research Review: Positive Adjustment to Adversity–Trajectories of Minimal–Impact Resilience and Emergent Resilience." Journal of Child Psychology and Psychiatry 54, no. 4 (2013): 378-401.

Soto, Christopher J. "How Replicable Are Links Between Personality Traits and Consequential Life Outcomes? The Life Outcomes of Personality Replication Project." Psychological Science 30, no. 5 (2019): 711-727.

Bleidorn, Wiebke, Patrick L. Hill, Mitja D. Back, Jaap J. A. Denissen, Marie Hennecke, Christopher J. Hopwood, Markus Jokela, et al. "The Policy Relevance of Personality Traits." American Psychologist 74, no. 9 (2019): 1056-1067.

CHAPTER 8

1. The importance of sharing goals with supportive others:
   - This study found that sharing goals with higher-status individuals increased goal commitment and performance, supporting the chapter's emphasis on telling trusted friends about your goals.
   - Klein, H. J., Lount, R. B., Park, H. M., & Linford, B. J. (2020). When goals are known: The effects of audience relative status on goal commitment and performance. Journal of Applied Psychology, 105(4), 372-389.

2. The power of accountability in achieving goals:
   - This research demonstrates how accountability mechanisms like implementation intentions can improve goal achievement, aligning with the chapter's focus on accountability partnerships.
   - Oettingen, G., Kappes, H. B., Guttenberg, K. B., & Gollwitzer, P. M. (2015). Self-regulation of time management: Mental contrasting with implementation intentions. European Journal of Social Psychology, 45(2), 218-229.

3. The impact of supportive relationships on personal growth: This influential article presents a comprehensive model of "thriving through relationships" that expands our understanding of how social support contributes to personal growth and well-being. Feeney and Collins propose that supportive relationships promote thriving in two key contexts: during adversity and when pursuing life opportunities. They introduce two corresponding

support functions: "source of strength" support for coping with challenges, and "relational catalyst" support for personal growth and goal pursuit.
- ○ Feeney, B. C., & Collins, N. L. (2015). A new look at social support: A theoretical perspective on thriving through relationships. Personality and Social Psychology Review, 19(2), 113-147.

4. Social support and goal achievement:
   - ○ Research has shown that social support significantly enhances goal pursuit and attainment. A meta-analysis published in Psychological Bulletin demonstrated the positive impact of social support on various outcomes, including goal achievement.
   - ○ Holt-Lunstad, J., Smith, T. B., & Layton, J. B. (2010). Social relationships and mortality risk: A meta-analytic review. PLoS Medicine, 7(7), e1000316.

5. The role of self-disclosure in personal growth:
   - ○ Studies have shown that sharing personal goals and challenges with others can lead to increased self-awareness and personal growth. Research published in the Journal of Personality and Social Psychology found that self-disclosure can lead to improved well-being and stronger social connections.
   - ○ Jourard, S. M. (1971). The transparent self. New York: Van Nostrand Reinhold.

6. The impact of supportive relationships on resilience:
   - ○ Research has demonstrated that supportive relationships can enhance an individual's resilience in facing challenges. A study published in the

journal Development and Psychopathology found that supportive relationships are a key factor in developing resilience.
- ○ Masten, A. S., & Cicchetti, D. (2016). Resilience in development: Progress and transformation. Developmental Psychopathology, 1-63.

ADDITIONAL REFERENCE MATERIAL

Oppong, Thomas. "The Accountability Effect: A Simple Way to Achieve Your Goals and Boost Your Performance." Medium, January 4, 2017. https://medium.com/the-mission/the-accountability-effect-a-simple-way-to-achieve-your-goals-and-boost-your-performance-8fb07a94d01a.

Sheldon, Kennon M., and Andrew J. Elliot. "Goal Striving, Need Satisfaction, and Longitudinal Well-Being: The Self-Concordance Model." Journal of Personality and Social Psychology 76, no. 3 (1999): 482-497.

Jourard, Sidney M. The Transparent Self. New York: Van Nostrand Reinhold, 1971.

Masten, Ann S., and Dante Cicchetti. "Resilience in Development: Progress and Transformation." Developmental Psychopathology 4 (2016): 1-63.

CHAPTER 9

1. On the importance of resilience and overcoming hardship: This comprehensive book examines the biological and psychological factors that contribute to resilience, aligning with the chapter's emphasis on developing resilience to overcome challenges.
   - Southwick, S. M., & Charney, D. S. (2018). Resilience: The science of mastering life's greatest challenges. Cambridge University Press.

2. Regarding growth mindset and its impact on mental health: This meta-analysis supports the chapter's discussion on how adopting a growth mindset can positively influence mental health and resilience.
   - Burnette, J. L., Knouse, L. E., Vavra, D. T., O'Boyle, E., & Brooks, M. A. (2020). Growth mindsets and psychological distress: A meta-analysis. Clinical Psychology Review, 77, 101816.

3. On the role of positive emotions in building resilience: This study aligns with the chapter's emphasis on reframing perspective and using positive emotions to overcome challenges.
   - Tugade, M. M., & Fredrickson, B. L. (2004). Resilient individuals use positive emotions to bounce back from negative emotional experiences. Journal of Personality and Social Psychology, 86(2), 320-333.

4. Regarding the importance of social support in building resilience: This research supports the chapter's discussion on leveraging support systems to overcome hardships.

- Ozbay, F., Johnson, D. C., Dimoulas, E., Morgan, C. A., Charney, D., & Southwick, S. (2007). "Social support and resilience to stress: from neurobiology to clinical practice." Psychiatry, 4(5), 35-40. This research supports the chapter's discussion on leveraging support systems to overcome hardships.

5. On developing resilience through practice:
    - Joyce, S., Shand, F., Tighe, J., Laurent, S. J., Bryant, R. A., & Harvey, S. B. (2018). "Road to resilience: a systematic review and meta-analysis of resilience training programmes and interventions." BMJ Open, 8(6), e017858.

ADDITIONAL RESEARCH MATERIAL

Bonanno, George A., Maren Westphal, and Anthony D. Mancini. "Resilience to Loss and Potential Trauma." Annual Review of Clinical Psychology 7 (2011): 511-535.

Dweck, Carol S. Mindset: The New Psychology of Success. New York: Random House, 2006.

Fishbach, Ayelet, and Ravi Dhar. "Goals as Excuses or Guides: The Liberating Effect of Perceived Goal Progress on Choice." Journal of Consumer Research 32, no. 3 (2005): 370-377.

Norem, Julie K., and Edward C. Chang. "The Positive Psychology of Negative Thinking." Journal of Clinical Psychology 58, no. 9 (2002): 993-1001.

Holt-Lunstad, Julianne, Timothy B. Smith, and J. Bradley Layton. "Social Relationships and Mortality Risk: A Meta-Analytic Review." PLoS Medicine 7, no. 7 (2010): e1000316.

CHAPTER 10

1. Celebrating achievements and self-efficacy: This seminal work by Bandura introduces the concept of self-efficacy, which is closely related to the chapter's emphasis on remembering past victories to build confidence for future challenges.
   - Bandura, A. (1977). Self-efficacy: Toward a unifying theory of behavioral change. Psychological Review, 84(2), 191-215.

2. The power of small wins:
   - A study published in the Harvard Business Review found that making progress in meaningful work is the single most important factor in boosting emotions, motivation, and perceptions during a workday.
   - Amabile, Teresa M., and Steven J. Kramer. "The Power of Small Wins." Harvard Business Review 89, no. 5 (2011): 70-80.

3. Positive reinforcement and goal achievement:
   - This article by Bandura and Locke examines the relationship between self-efficacy, goal setting, and performance. The authors present a comprehensive review of research, including nine meta-analyses, that strongly supports the positive effects of self-efficacy beliefs and personal goals on motivation and performance.
   - Bandura, Albert, and Edwin A. Locke. "Negative Self-Efficacy and Goal Effects Revisited." Journal of Applied Psychology 88, no. 1 (2003): 87-99.

Additional Reference

Oettingen, Gabriele, Hyeon-ju Pak, and Karoline Schnetter. "Self-Regulation of Goal Setting: Turning Free Fantasies About the Future into Binding Goals." Journal of Personality and Social Psychology 80, no. 5 (2001): 736-753.

Emmons, Robert A., and Michael E. McCullough. "Counting Blessings Versus Burdens: An Experimental Investigation of Gratitude and Subjective Well-Being in Daily Life." Journal of Personality and Social Psychology 84, no. 2 (2003): 377-389.

Jeannerod, Marc. "Neural Simulation of Action: A Unifying Mechanism for Motor Cognition." NeuroImage 14, no. 1 (2001): S103-S109.

CHAPTER 11

1. The power of reaching goals: This influential article explores the complex relationship between subgoals and overarching goals in human behavior. Fishbach, Dhar, and Zhang investigate how the pursuit of subgoals can either complement or substitute for the pursuit of broader, superordinate goals. Their research demonstrates that the accessibility of the superordinate goal plays a crucial role in determining this relationship.
    - Fishbach, Ayelet, Ravi Dhar, and Ying Zhang. "Subgoals as Substitutes or Complements: The Role of Goal Accessibility." Journal of Personality and Social Psychology 91, no. 2 (2006): 232-242.

2. This meta-analysis examines the relationship between self-efficacy and work-related performance across 114

studies (k = 157, N = 21,616). Stajkovic and Luthans found a significant weighted average correlation of $G(r+) = .38$ between self-efficacy and work-related performance, indicating a moderate to strong positive relationship.
- Stajkovic, Alexander D., and Fred Luthans. "Self-Efficacy and Work-Related Performance: A Meta-Analysis." Psychological Bulletin 124, no. 2 (1998): 240-261.

3. The Power of Small Wins:
    - "The Importance of Small Wins" by Sonya Looney (2022) emphasizes how small victories are crucial building blocks for progress, motivation, and confidence.
    - Looney, Sonya. "The Importance of Small Wins." Sonya Looney (blog). Accessed October 18, 2024. https://sonyalooney.com/the-importance-of-small-wins/.

4. Success Breeding Further Success:
    - "Success breeds success: Physiological, psychological, and economic perspectives of momentum (hot hand)" by Morgulev (2023) explores how initial success can lead to subsequent successes.
    - Elia Morgulev, Success breeds success: Physiological, psychological, and economic perspectives of momentum (hot hand), Asian Journal of Sport and Exercise Psychology, Volume 3, Issue 1, 2023, Pages 3-7, ISSN 2667-2391, https://doi.org/10.1016/j.ajsep.2023.04.002.

5. Neurological Basis of Momentum:
    - "Reinforcement learning in professional basketball players" by Neiman and Loewenstein (2011) investigates the neurological underpinnings of momentum in professional athletes.
    - Tal Neiman & Yonatan Loewenstein, 2011. "Reinforcement learning in professional basketball players," Discussion Paper Series dp593, The Federmann Center for the Study of Rationality, the Hebrew University, Jerusalem.

ADDITIONAL RESEARCH MATERIAL

Jeannerod, Marc. "Neural Simulation of Action: A Unifying Mechanism for Motor Cognition." NeuroImage 14, no. 1 (2001): S103-S109.

Taylor, Shelley E., Lien B. Pham, Inna D. Rivkin, and David A. Armor. "Harnessing the Imagination: Mental Simulation, Self-Regulation, and Coping." American Psychologist 53, no. 4 (1998): 429-439.

Locke, Edwin A., and Gary P. Latham. "Building a Practically Useful Theory of Goal Setting and Task Motivation: A 35-Year Odyssey." American Psychologist 57, no. 9 (2002): 705-717.

Dweck, Carol S. Mindset: The New Psychology of Success. New York: Random House, 2006.

CHAPTER 12

1. The power of visualization in achieving goals:
   - "Imagining Success: Multiple Achievement Goals and the Effectiveness of Imagery" (Bernier & Fournier, 2016)
   - Blankert T, Hamstra MR. Imagining Success: Multiple Achievement Goals and the Effectiveness of Imagery. Basic Appl Soc Psych. 2017 Jan 2; 39(1):60-67. doi: 10.1080/01973533.2016.1255947. Epub 2016 Dec 7. PMID: 28366970; PMCID: PMC5351796.

2. The impact of positive thinking on success: This article discusses how a positive mindset leads to improved mental health, increased productivity, enhanced relationships, and better physical health.
   - "The Impact of a Positive Mindset on Personal and Professional Success" (Psychology Today, n.d.) Life Coach Training Institute. "The Impact of a Positive Mindset on Personal and Professional Success." Accessed October 18, 2024. https://lifecoachtraining.co/the-impact-of-a-positive-mindset-on-personal-and-professional-success/.

3. Setting SMART goals:
   - This article outlines the SMART goal-setting framework (Specific, Measurable, Achievable, Relevant, Time-bound) as part of effective visualization techniques.
   - "8 Visualization Strategies That Make Your Goals a Reality," (Leaders.com, n.d.)
   - Leaders Media. "8 Visualization Strategies That Make Your Goals a Reality." Accessed October 18,

2024. https://leaders.com/articles/personal-growth/visualization/.

4. The relationship between organizational culture and success:
    - This study found that organizational culture is significantly correlated with leadership behavior and job satisfaction.
    - "Relationship between Organizational Culture, Leadership Behavior and Job Satisfaction" (Tsai, 2011)
    - Tsai Y. Relationship between organizational culture, leadership behavior and job satisfaction. BMC Health Serv Res. 2011 May 14; 11:98. doi: 10.1186/1472-6963-11-98. PMID: 21569537; PMCID: PMC3123547.

5. The importance of growth mindset in education:
    - This paper reviews the theoretical and empirical origins of mindset culture and its potential to reduce educational inequalities.
    - Hecht, C.A., Murphy, M.C., Dweck, C.S. *et al.* Shifting the mindset culture to address global educational disparities. *npj Sci. Learn.* **8**, 29 (2023). https://doi.org/10.1038/s41539-023-00181-y

6. The evolution of mindset research:
    - This article offers perspectives on mindset research across two eras, discussing how it has evolved to address underachievement through field experiments and interventions.
    - Dweck, C. S., & Yeager, D. S. (2019). Mindsets: A View From Two Eras. Perspectives on Psychological Science, 14(3), 481-496. https://doi.org/10.1177/1745691618804166

POSSUM PICKIN'S: FINGER-LICKIN' RECIPES FOR YOUR NEXT ROADKILL RODEO

ARKANSAS POSSUM PIE RECIPE

PREP TIME: 20 minutes
COOK TIME: 25 minutes
ADDITIONAL TIME: 4 hours
TOTAL TIME: 4 hours 45 minutes
COURSE: Dessert
CUISINE: American
SERVINGS: 10

Arkansas Possum Pie is a creamy, layered chocolate and cream cheese pie in a pecan shortbread crust that is sure to please!

INGREDIENTS

Pecan Shortbread Crust

- 1 cup **all-purpose flour**
- ½ cup **salted butter**
- ¼ cup **brown sugar**

- ¾ cup **pecans**, chopped

Pudding Layer

- 1 cup **granulated sugar**
- ⅓ cup **natural unsweetened cocoa powder**
- 3 Tablespoons **cornstarch**
- 2 Tablespoons **all-purpose flour**
- Pinch of **salt**
- 3 **egg yolks**
- 2 cups **whole milk**
- 2 Tablespoons **salted butter**
- 1 teaspoon **pure vanilla extract**

Cream Cheese Layer

- 8 ounces **cream cheese**, softened
- ½ cup **heavy whipping cream**
- 2 Tablespoons **powdered sugar**
- ½ teaspoon **pure vanilla extract**

Whipped Cream Topping

- 2 Tablespoons **heavy cream**
- ½ cup **powdered sugar**
- 1-2 Tablespoons **chopped pecans**
- **Grated chocolate**

Cook Mode

INSTRUCTIONS

Crust

- Preheat the oven to 350°F. Melt the butter, then combine the butter, flour, brown sugar, and pecans by stirring with a fork. Press into the bottom of a 9-inch **pie plate** *(affiliate link)*.
- Bake for about 15-20 minutes, just until the crust begins to brown around the edges. Remove from oven and cool completely.

Chocolate Layer

- Combine the sugar, cocoa powder, cornstarch, flour, and salt in a medium saucepan and whisk well.
- In a separate bowl, combine the egg yolks and milk and whisk well, then add to the sugar and cocoa powder mixture in the saucepan, whisking to combine.
- Cook over medium heat, whisking constantly until pudding begins to thicken and bubble, about 7-10 minutes. Remove from the heat and add the butter and vanilla, stirring just until the butter is melted and combined. Transfer the chocolate pudding to a shallow bowl and cover with a plastic wrap directly on the surface of the pudding to prevent a skin from forming, then refrigerate for 30 minutes to help the filling cool down.
- When the filling has mostly cooled down, remove the plastic wrap and stir, then spread over the cream cheese layer. Cover the pie with plastic wrap, then refrigerate for 4 hours until set.

Cream Cheese Filling

- In a medium bowl, mix the cream cheese, powdered sugar, and heavy cream using a hand mixer until smooth. Spread over the bottom of the cooled pecan pie crust.

Whipped Cream Topping

- Beat the heavy cream with the powdered sugar and vanilla using a hand mixer until whipped cream forms and holds its shape when batters are removed. Spread the whipped cream over the top of the chocolate pudding layer and sprinkle with a handful of chopped pecans and chocolate shavings before slicing and serving.

SUSAN'S ARKANSAS POSSUM PIE

Crust:

- 1 cup Flour
- 1 stick Butter
- 1 cup chopped Pecans

Filling:

- 1 (8 oz) Cream Cheese
- 1 cup frozen Whipped Topping, thawed
- 1 cup Confectioners' Sugar

Pudding:

- 2– "4 serving boxes" Instant Chocolate Pudding
- 3 cups cold milk

- Topping:
- 8-ounce carton Cool Whip

Directions:

Crust:

1. Preheat oven to 350°F.
2. Mix flour, butter, and pecans together with a pastry blender or fork.
3. Press into 9 x 13 inch baking dish.
4. Bake for 20 minutes.
5. Cool completely.

Filling:

1. In a mixing bowl, cream cheese and sugar until well blended
2. Add whipped topping and stir ingredients together.
3. Carefully spread over the cooled crust.

Pudding Filling:

1. In a bowl, mix pudding packages and milk together with a wire whisk until well blended.
2. Allow to sit for 5 minutes.
3. Carefully spread over cream cheese layer.

Topping:

1. Carefully spread remaining whipped topping over chocolate pudding layer.
2. Refrigerate until serving time.

EAT THE POSSUM PERSONALITY QUIZ

PERSONALITY TEST

Instructions: For each statement, choose the option that best describes you:

1 = Strongly Disagree
2 = Disagree
3 = Neutral
4 = Agree
5 = Strongly Agree

1. I enjoy solving complex puzzles and brain teasers.
2. I have strong beliefs about right and wrong.
3. I can easily tell when someone is upset, even if they don't say anything.
4. I love being the center of attention at parties.
5. I often act without thinking things through.
6. I daydream a lot and have a vivid imagination.
7. I set high goals for myself and work hard to achieve them.
8. I trust my gut feelings when making decisions.

9. I'm always eager to try new things and visit new places.
10. I need solid proof before I believe something.
11. I like to have a clear plan for my day.
12. I'm good at helping people resolve their arguments.
13. I enjoy thinking about abstract ideas and theories.
14. I stand up for what I believe in, even if others disagree.
15. I often put others' needs before my own.
16. I can easily convince people to see things my way.
17. I don't like following a strict routine.
18. I often think about the meaning of life and my purpose.
19. I'm very competitive and always strive to be the best.
20. I'm good at reading between the lines in conversations.
21. I'm always looking for my next exciting adventure.
22. I prefer to have all the facts before making a decision.
23. I like to keep my belongings neat and organized.
24. People often come to me for advice or to talk about their problems.
25. I enjoy breaking down complex problems into smaller parts.
26. I have a strong sense of duty and responsibility.
27. I can easily put myself in someone else's shoes.
28. I'm good at motivating and inspiring others.
29. I often get bored with doing things the same way all the time.
30. I enjoy exploring deep, philosophical questions.
31. I push myself to achieve more, even when others think I've done enough.
32. I often know things without being able to explain how I know them.
33. I love the thrill of trying something new and potentially risky.

34. I need to understand how things work before I accept them.
35. I prefer to have clear rules and guidelines to follow.
36. I'm often called upon to mediate conflicts between others.
37. I enjoy analyzing data and finding patterns.
38. I have a strong moral code that guides my actions.
39. I'm very in tune with other people's emotions.
40. I'm comfortable speaking in front of large groups.
41. I like to shake things up and challenge the status quo.
42. I spend a lot of time reflecting on my thoughts and feelings.
43. I set ambitious goals for myself and work tirelessly to achieve them.
44. I often have hunches that turn out to be correct.
45. I'm always on the lookout for new and exciting experiences.
46. I'm skeptical of new ideas until I see proof that they work.
47. I like to plan things in advance and stick to the plan.
48. I'm good at finding compromises that make everyone happy.
49. I enjoy learning about complex scientific theories.
50. I have strong opinions about social and political issues.

SCORING MECHANISM

To calculate your scores, sum your ratings for the following questions:

1. Analytical Alex: 1, 13, 25, 37, 49
2. Principled Paula: 2, 14, 26, 38, 50
3. Empathetic Emma: 3, 15, 27, 39, 24
4. Charismatic Charlie: 4, 16, 28, 40, 19

5. Spontaneous Sam: 5, 17, 29, 41, 33
6. Contemplative Cory: 6, 18, 30, 42, 20
7. Ambitious Ava: 7, 19, 31, 43, 7
8. Intuitive Ian (Discerner): 8, 20, 32, 44, 8
9. Adventurous Andy: 9, 21, 33, 45, 21
10. Cautious Cathy: 10, 22, 34, 46, 22
11. Diplomatic Dan: 12, 24, 36, 48, 36
12. Organized Olivia: 11, 23, 35, 47, 23

Your highest score indicates your dominant personality type. If you have tied scores, you may have a blend of those personality types.

RESULTS INTERPRETATION

Your dominant personality type is the one with the highest score. Here's a brief description of each type:

Analytical Alex: You enjoy solving complex problems and thinking deeply about issues.

Principled Paula: You have strong values and a clear sense of right and wrong.

Empathetic Emma: You're highly attuned to others' emotions and often put their needs first.

Charismatic Charlie: You're outgoing, persuasive, and enjoy being the center of attention.

Spontaneous Sam: You're impulsive, enjoy novelty, and often challenge the status quo.

Contemplative Cory: You have a rich inner world and enjoy exploring deep, philosophical questions.

Ambitious Ava: You set high goals for yourself and work tirelessly to achieve them.

Intuitive Ian (Discerner): You trust your gut feelings and often have insights you can't easily explain.

Adventurous Andy: You love new experiences and are always seeking your next exciting adventure.

Cautious Cathy: You're skeptical of new ideas and need solid evidence before accepting them.

Diplomatic Dan: You're skilled at finding common ground and resolving conflicts.

Organized Olivia: You prefer structure, clear rules, and having everything in order.

ABOUT THE AUTHOR

Dr. John Utley isn't your average possum-eater. Armed with a doctorate in Strategic Christian Ministry from Liberty University, he's been wrangling life's toughest challenges for over three decades. As a pastor, consultant, and life coach, he's helped folks face their personal "possums" head-on, from addiction to organizational upheaval.

Don't let his academic credentials fool you – Dr. Utley's approach is as down-to-earth as a country barbecue. He's a family man who knows that sometimes, the hardest possum to eat is the one sitting at your own dinner table. His unique blend of biblical wisdom and practical advice has made him the go-to guy for those ready to tackle their biggest fears.

Whether he's preaching from the pulpit or coaching a CEO, Dr. Utley's message remains the same: it's time to grab your fork and dig in. With "EAT THE POSSUM," he's serving up a heaping plate of life-changing insights, proving that with the right seasoning, even the most daunting challenges can become a feast of personal growth.

So, are you ready to face your fears, overcome your obstacles, and discover just how tasty transformation can be? Dr. Utley's here to show you that sometimes, the path to extraordinary things starts with a bite of something unexpected. Find out more at www.eatthepossum.com

#eatthepossum